MUSIC HABITS

The mental game of electronic music production

Finish songs fast, beat procrastination, and find your creative flow

By Jason Timothy

Table of Contents

Introduction

Music Production can be an elusive art form for many, and the challenges that face someone who is new to this can easily create overwhelm and lead to complete paralysis. The goal of this book, is to cover music production from many different angles in a way that will change your thinking on the subject and build your confidence.

Music making is a very mental and psychological game, and more often than not, all the technical stuff can hold you back from achieving your goals if you don't have the right creative habits in place first.

With all the information available with a simple Google search, I wanted to really get to the heart of things that aren't being discussed nearly enough. I want to clear out all the garbage you may have been told and replace it with the essentials you can put to immediate use. Many people new to music may dive into forums and mindlessly watch video tutorials attempting to gather more and more information until they think they have enough to get going (hint: you *never* feel like you know enough).

That would be like reading a whole encyclopedia and then being asked to recall only the important things that will get you from point A to point B. Even worse, much of the information you get will contradict the last thing you read. It's like finding a needle in a haystack only to be told it's the wrong needle. There is a much better approach. It's an approach that doesn't require you to know a lot to get started. You only need to know enough to get to the next step in your process.

There is truly nothing stopping you from becoming a music producer. The ones who are successful now are the ones who started from nothing and chipped away at it until they found a way to express their unique voice. There are no gatekeepers making decisions on who is worthy and who isn't. The determining factor is you, your habits and your confidence in yourself.

This book can be read from start to finish, or as a "choose your own adventure", going directly to what you think can help you most right now. Don't get caught up thinking you have to devour *everything* before getting started. That isn't necessary, and isn't the point of the book.

The core concepts in the book will come up time & time again which should help you retain them & be able to recall them when the need arrives. By exploring these concepts from several angles you should gain a broad view of their many uses.

My hope is that this book is used as a toolbox. You simply find the right tool that moves you forward and get back to work. So few people, who have more than enough information in their heads, ever start. Of those who *do* start, even fewer finish what they started and are satisfied with the results. I want you to be in that small group of finishers.

Let's   get   started.

10 golden rules

If you are new to music production, or even if you've been poking around for a while, there are a number of things that you haven't been told about making music. Depending on what angle you are taking to get into the music production game, you are likely either over or under preparing for what lies ahead.

Sadly, many suffer from what they consider to be complete failure and thus give up. It is my belief that if they had this information ahead of time, they probably would have had the power to move through the rough spots. The following are ten things I certainly wish I had known when I started (or even after ten years in!)

1. **Your first attempts at making music won't be great, and that's the way it should be**

   One of the biggest mistakes an aspiring producer can make is to think their next song is going to be the song that not only changes their lives, but changes music history. Unfortunately, these are the high expectations and pressure they put on themselves, and this is the reason they never finish anything. Nothing you make the first time around can compete with the producers who have churned out hundreds or even thousands of songs.

   If you sit there for a year or more struggling with making your first song the hit of the century, you are missing the opportunity that creating many imperfect songs can bring you. The truth is that you need to finish a good ten to twenty songs before you start to find your groove. This might seem daunting for perfectionist, but if you can put aside perfection and just call a project done when you've reached the tip of your current skill level, you'll find yourself improving at a dramatically faster rate. Plus, as your production and listening skills get better, you can always go back and revisit old songs for improvements that now seem   obvious   to   you.

2. Nobody creates in a constant peak state

Peak states of consciousness, also called flow, is considered to be the most desired state of being a human can experience. Extreme athletes and adventurists don't risk their lives because they are crazy. It's because being on the edge is the only way to create these flow states. Nobody can experience these states constantly.

And when I say nobody, I mean it. The reason for this is that peak states of creativity follow a pattern which involves lulls and frustration. Its two sides of the same coin, and you simply can't have one without the other. If you aren't putting yourself at the edge of your capabilities and risking failure, your level of focus simply won't be intense enough to put you into this peak state of mind.

If you are a multi-tasker or tend to surround yourself with distractions, you will have no chance of reaching this state. Peak creativity states make the whole world fade away and you experience "now" in a way that can't really be explained unless you have been there.

Great artists have taught themselves how to get into this state more often than others, but still understand that 90% of the time all artists have to push themselves to do the work, regardless of how they feel. In fact, as I wrote this I was interrupted and brought into a whole conversation that I had to politely exit. It will now take me a bit of time to get back into my flow, even though it wasn't a "peak" flow. Regardless, the show must go on and so must you. Don't wait for the right time. Peak states only come to those who are willing to do the work regardless.

3. Most of what you think you need to know, doesn't matter

So many artists have this belief that they can't start making music with what they know right now. Because of this fear of creating, they over prepare. They end up wasting hundreds of hours watching every tutorial outlining tips for every style of music, and diving deep into music theory.

What they don't realize is that most of this information will fall right back out of their head and never make it into their tool box. On top of that, they are getting so many opposing pieces of advice that all this information causes more confusion than it does benefits.

As a rule, a new producer should be spending 80% of their time making music and only 20% (at most) spent learning new techniques. I recommend you take your own skills as far as you possibly can, and only then do you search out the one or two tutorials that will get you over that creative hump so you can reach the next level in your music making.

This is the only way you will retain what you have learned as well as the only way you will keep yourself focused on actually music making. Don't get yourself caught up in the information trap for the wrong reasons.

4. Most of the tools you think you need, you don't

Many producers, new and old, join groups and forums related to their musical style or DAW of choice. I believe it is smart to interact with likeminded people, but be warned. The time people are spending in these forums is time they probably should be using to make great music. This lack of focus on actually working on your music can become contagious, as everyone in the group lets everyone else off the hook.

Then there are the "know-it-alls". These are the people who are pissed off that their amazing talents haven't boosted them into the stratosphere of fame and glory. These people are better than you and want you to know it.

"Oh, you're using *that* compressor? That thing sounds like dog shit! If you aren't using xyz plugin or *this* piece of hardware, you might as well pack it in."

Pretty soon you are spending all of your song writing time searching forums, discussing 10 different points of view on what compressor you need to have to be taken seriously by your peers.

Stop it. *Stop it.* STOP IT!

Yes, there are some amazing plugin's out there, but the truth is, if you learn how to use a certain tool inside and out, you can usually get great results. I personally use mostly internal plugins from my DAW of choice (Ableton). I've heard many people tell me Logic effects are better, and although I wouldn't disagree, I've found a way to get the job done quickly and efficiently with the tools I have, and so far, the type of plugin's I use has not affected getting my tracks signed and reaching the charts one single bit.

At the end of the day, the person that finishes the most songs wins every time. Focus on that.

5. Your habits count more than your knowledge

Once again, you need to stop thinking you need to know everything. I've personally gone that route. In the past, I was able to teach people how to use music software inside and out and they would take a few chosen gems and run with them, while disregarding much of the information they didn't need right now. Good on them, they were finishing music, and at the time I wasn't. Lesson learned.

If you want to be a successful songwriter or producer, you should first concentrate on your habits far before your knowledge. If you haven't instilled the habits that will force you to work on music daily, your knowledge won't matter.

Frankly it's a bit stupid to keep adding tools to your already oversized toolbox if you are never going to sit your ass down and use them.

You will get *far* more benefit by creating the habit of sitting in from of your DAW of choice for fifteen minutes a day, even if you don't write a thing, than you will from force feeding your brain with more "knowledge".

If you ever want to create a creative flow, it comes from clearing your mind, not stuffing it like that closet you don't show any of your guests.

6. Everything you want comes through people

People are more important than knowledge. Look around at all of those highly successful people. Are they all there because they are geniuses? No way.

Everything you want (outside of your personal spiritual growth) is going to require relationships. You simply can't stay locked out from the world, making great music, and expect that to be enough. You are going to have to interact, communicate and share your value in trade for the value of others.

If you think you are above promoting yourself (in the most ethical way of course) and sharing you with the world, the world will never have the opportunity to appreciate who you are, and what it is you do so well. Anyone who tells you otherwise, is lying to you.

7. You don't have to be miserable to make good music

Man, if I hadn't wasted all those years with the "artist" mentality, I might have gotten more done and enjoyed myself a whole lot more.

You don't need to fabricate a difficult, dark and addicted lifestyle to be great. I'm not saying that getting out of your head every once in a while can't be beneficial. It's not popular to say this, but sometimes the drugs do work, at least for a little bit. Gladly, I did my share and got out of it before doing myself much permanent damage.

I can reflect on those experiences from a sober state of mind and say with complete conviction that I am ten times more productive as a sober person (who has the occasional beer). Don't follow your fellow musicians down the rabbit hole too far, or you will fuck yourself, your creativity and your productivity.

Have experiences and make music, but always give your music top priority. The "lifestyle" is largely bullshit anyway. Don't believe the hype.

8. Musicianship is optional

I've spoken out many times of my happiness in being a non-musician, or at least my happiness of not letting it get in the way of creating things I am proud of. So many great songwriters are not the best musicians, and many of the best electronic artists don't have a big musical background, and many of those who do found it a hindrance to creating outside the box at times.

A non-musician does not have a total lack of talent, it's just coming from another angle. The man who I consider to be the greatest engineer and one of the most celebrated artists is Brian Eno. All the music theory in the world wouldn't put me at his level of talent. He's responsible for some of the best works of David Bowie, U2, David Byrne, Coldplay (I know, I know), James and even Devo, not to mention his incredible work with Roxy Music.

For all of the incredible music he is responsible for, he still considers himself a crap musician. If you have a music background, wonderful, use it. If you don't, also wonderful, create from a different angle. You will never know your capabilities until you embrace them.

9. Time is the only difference from you and those who are now successful

Your musical heroes are not really heroes, they are arrows pointing in the direction of your own potential. Do not entertain the thought that "some have it and some don't". It's simply not true. The truth is that some people (unfortunately very few) work for it tirelessly and consistently until they get it. Some of the best artists actually took longer to get there than you would expect.

If you want to know whether you've got it in you or not, look at your daily habits, not your skill level.

10. Everybody steals

So many people are so fucking paranoid that they just sit there staring at their computer screen, like me wandering aimlessly in a supermarket trying to put a meal together. My god, if I couldn't steal recipes from people much more gifted in cooking than me, I'd be in even more trouble.

The truth is, that all of the music you hear is inspired by another musician, artist, poet or some abstract thing someone recognized as having a beauty that others might not have seen from that perspective.

That idea you are afraid to borrow was almost certainly inspired by someone else, if not completely stolen. Picasso, John Lennon and Steve Jobs, all considered to be creative innovators all are famously quoted for nicking ideas pretty blatantly. You think Led Zeppelin were innovators? I did too and I still love them, but if you do some research, I'm sure you'll be shocked.

Stealing ideas is how artists constantly fuel their own creativity. Letting go of the fear of being completely original will actually set you free and make you more creative, not less. Use samples, presets, loops, quotes, or even steal from your own past ideas. Nothing you can steal will be put back together quite like the source you got it from.

We are all human filters. This means that no matter what we borrow or steal, it still has to run through our unique set of parameters before it gets spit back out as our own art. Drop the fear and use everything around you when you create. It's liberating.

Time

*Not enough time for music? Bullsh*t!*

This has been a long time coming and it's time we had a one on one sit down.

I've been spending years telling people how they *can* make some serious strides in their music making. While many feel that initial boost of energy and motivation, a large percentage start telling me why they *can't* do it. Since whatever you say to yourself and others ends up being the truth in your reality, it seems extremely counterproductive to allow anything but thoughts of what *is* possible into your mind.

Your excuses are largely laziness. This is not to say that you are a lazy person in general, as many of you have very busy lives. Where laziness comes into play is in changing your routine and better managing your time for your creative endeavors. Let me explain.

Your brain is usually running on autopilot. 90% of the things you do today are things you did yesterday, and the day before. This of course includes breathing and heartbeat, but also includes very deeply ingrained habits. Your brain relies on these autopilot habits to conserve energy. Any type of new challenges that require a new set of thinking skills is going to be rejected pretty fast to free up energy resources.

Thinking requires energy

To think a new thought or to solve a new problem or to explore a new interest is comparable to getting an airplane in the air. You have to put in a lot of consistent energy to reach a comfortable flight level. You often have to pull energy from other sources temporarily to get lift off. Lift off is when your new action becomes habit and gets added to your autopilot, requiring much less energy.

Making music is the ultimate process of repeatedly facing new difficult challenges that the brain doesn't want to give energy to. Ever notice how much you want to take a nap or just gel out when you are trying to work on something new?

I assert that the real reason many of you start slacking or give up all together is that you haven't put in enough consistent effort to change your current challenges into solutions on autopilot.

Why tutorials can be bad for you

You may think I am shooting myself in the foot here since I make tutorials for a living, but I see what I do differently. My true purpose is not to get you to watch tutorials or read my books, (although I appreciate both), it's to empower creative people to find their spark and transform themselves into productive and successful music makers.

Tutorials can be the invisible enemy disguising itself as your friend, especially when you aren't feeling confident in your current skill set. Instead of fighting through a track and learning from personal experience, you convince yourself that you are being productive because you are teaching yourself new tricks. Unfortunately, unless you put to *immediate* use, you'll forget 80% of what you watched.

To back up this claim, I have found myself watching some of my own tutorials to remember a technique I shared. True story! See, we only have a good memory of the techniques we *put to use regularly*, not the ones stuck dormant in our heads.

Remember, working on your song is an active experience. It's putting something new into the world. Learning is very passive and it is taking something that already exists in the world. Can you see the major difference?

Opening your DAW and listening to your 8 bar loop for twenty minutes is NOT making music. It's just procrastinating.

Your big excuse: not enough time

Well, of course you don't have any time. You have a busy life and you are spending all your music making time doing one or more of the following:

Batching

Is there something you do every day? Sometimes 5 or 6 times a day? I bet it breaks your focus and takes you a good amount of time to get back into your groove. Is it possible to batch your email and Facebook to just ten-fifteen minutes once in the day time and once a night? That alone can give you up to an hour of productivity a day.

Do you spend a lot of time in the kitchen preparing food? Is it possible you can prepare certain foods all on one day that you can enjoy for up to a week? I personally cut up a week's worth of salad stuff and put them into plastic containers, so every day it takes no more than two-three minutes to make a salad. I do this for steamed veggies, rice or beans as well. Huge timesaver.

Take a look at what daily errands you might be doing that can be batched into just once or twice a week.

Welcome back to your music life!

As I said from the beginning, your excuses are bullshit and the solutions are plenty. There are really only two things left to do:

.1   Create time

.2   Create your own dent in the universe.

Spend less time on your music for more creative output

If you are at all like me, you have gone through (or are going through) some creative struggles. You simply aren't carving out the time you need to get any real music done. Does the idea of starting a new project seem like a waste, since you feel you never have the time to dive in deep enough to get anything accomplished?

I know exactly how you feel. A while back I made a thirty day commitment to myself to work on music two hours a day, every day. It didn't matter what I was doing, as long as I was creating. I figured this type of discipline would be exactly what I needed to start purging through all of my unfinished ideas.

This went well for the first 5 days and I was pretty motivated the first three days of them. Then "life" happened and something kept me from meeting my day's goal. From there I felt much less committed to my goal of thirty days. I had a couple spurts of creative action, but felt like I had already failed on my commitment. From there, I really dropped the ball for most of the month.

Although I would consider revisiting this goal, I feel this original goal just wasn't very realistic for me (I say "for me" because some of you may feel this is pretty reasonable. If that is the case, go for it!).

Now I have a different approach for pretty much any goal.

Think of it like exercise. The idea is to set a *habit* first instead of thinking about maximum production and output. My new idea is to set a goal simple enough that it would be ridiculous to not be able to accomplish it every day. The key here is *every day*. Not five days a week, not every other day – *every day*. This is so important in habit forming.

When I decided I wanted to get in better shape, I decided that I would commit to twenty push-ups and fifty sit-ups. Nothing less, nothing more. This was pretty easy to accomplish, and only took up a few minutes of my time every day. Although I wasn't noticing much if any difference in my strength, the strength of my daily habit was quite noticeable.

As the habit became a no brainer, I decided to start challenging myself to do more sit-ups and push-ups, and then added a fairly easy weight routine. Soon enough I was not only noticing a difference, I couldn't even *think* of skipping a day. The point here is creating the habit first. Once that is in place, slowly build your resistance in small enough increments that it is challenging, but not so challenging that you would be tempted to skip a day.

So, back to music making

My proposal to you is to devote yourself to just *fifteen minutes a day*, every day, to music making. It doesn't matter what it is you do, but make sure you are creating in *some* way.

If you are away from your computer or away from home, perhaps you can pick up a friends acoustic guitar, write some lyrics or hum a melody into a portable recorder. Whatever the situation, wherever you are...*no more excuses*...**fifteen minutes**. That's all.

As you build up the habit and you start to look forward to the process, a few things will likely happen.

• Your mind will start tuning into being creative, and more ideas will start popping in your head.

• You will actually become more productive in fifteen minutes than most people are in an hour... this is the benefit of habits. Habits lead to greater efficiency.

• You may find yourself going way past your fifteen minute goal more and more often, but don't let yourself slide on the fifteen minutes you have to spend tomorrow.

I'm certain that if you follow this habit forming technique in your musical life as well as other aspects of your life, you'll find yourself with many more accomplishments than you likely thought possible for you!

Here's a slightly different creative approach you can feel free to try

Once you have your habit in place, you may want to create more urgency in your creativity. This can be done by putting a limit on your creativity each day.

Yes, I said to *limit* your time.

"I will only allow myself thirty minutes of music making today". This is a good way to keep your analytical left brain from second guessing everything you do, and create enough urgency to *accomplish much more in less time.*

Isn't *that* why death was created in the first place? If there was no death, very few of us would do much of anything, because there would always be tomorrow.

Don't wait until tomorrow, get started today and every day. Start small to form a habit, then build resistance once you have the habit   in   place.

Habits

Why Quantity is better than Quality

You've heard it over and over how the quality of your creative work is so much more important than quantity, but I think it's time we turn this belief system on its head. Not only is it wrong when making music, it can end up both crippling your creative output, and lessening the quality of your results.

I'm sure you can give me a hundred reasons why you shouldn't haphazardly throw creations out into the world, most of which would be making assumptions about what you are truly capable of. You would also be making an assumption that everything you complete needs to be shared with the world. It doesn't.

I don't believe that all creations are meant to be shared, but I do believe that creating a habit of not finishing songs becomes a big part of your creative process. If you quit working on a song when it gets difficult or tedious, you never build the tools and habits to get past this point, and you'll never finish anything you start.

Let's be honest. None of us wants to be a shitty artist. The desire to be great is deeply ingrained in each of us. The fear of sucking at something we are passionate about can either lead us to greatness or mediocrity, depending on our perspective.

Repetition makes you better at whatever habit is being repeated. This means that if you have the habit of quitting every time something isn't working out, you become a habitual quitter. On the other hand, if you are repeating the process of completing your work and accepting where you're at, you can turn your weaknesses into strengths.

Nobody starts off a black belt

Are you going to refuse to face an opponent until you're the best in your class? Is this supposed to save you the embarrassment of losing? That's a pretty stupid approach. Those who take this approach obviously haven't come to the realization that the only opponent is yourself, and that your only goal is to be better than you were yesterday. By taking any other approach, you are doomed to failing by default. Not taking action, or quitting before you reach your goal is failing yourself, and your true potential. I haven't heard of any great martial artists who didn't at one time get their asses handed to them. That is specifically how you learn and get better.

If you are refusing to finish a song because it's not as good as (fill in the blank of some artist who has failed their way to greatness), you are facing the wrong opponent. If you are expecting your first songs to be amazing, you will be grabbing at something you aren't tall enough to reach yet. The only way to grow, is to keep stretching yourself. Seeing through your failures to completion, and noticing improvements in each attempt is how you grow.

The secret to becoming great

If you seek *quantity over quality*, you will get both.

By creating the habit of seeing things through, you can't help but improve the quality of your work. Like I said earlier, the desire to be great is already wired into us. It's the natural outcome to repeated action.

You also become great by learning to make decisions quickly instead of over thinking the 10,000 options available to you at every moment. Through experience, you'll find that there are rarely wrong decisions, just better decisions. A wrong decision can often become a brave and unique technique with a few tweaks.

You know the cliché, *the only bad decisions are the ones you don't make*. This isn't surgery. Nobody gets hurt if you aren't perfect. Besides, perfection is boring and overrated.

Let's say you idolize Mozart and you put everything you do up to his work. If your goal is to sound as good as Mozart before you will consider a song complete or worth sharing, you're going to be doomed to mediocrity. Not because you have bad taste in music and a great artist to model yourself after, but that you will never be satisfied with your own work.

You'll never feel what it's like to have someone love your music, even if, in your eyes, it's not up to your standards. John Lennon (The Beatles) didn't like the sound of his own voice. Can you imagine if he had waited until he loved his own voice before sharing his music with the world? What a shame that would be.

Sound design vs. Workflow

Have you ever had a great song idea, but by the time you started attempting to create the sounds in your head you've lost the inspiration? If so, you are in good company. This happens to the best of us.

Although there is nothing wrong with creating music with pre-set sounds, it is often not as inspiring. Presets give you a great starting point, but sound design can give you those extra unexpected results that can take your music to the next level.

So what do I suggest for a better workflow?

Through conversations with other producers, I decided that it's best to create work sessions completely devoted to experimenting with sounds, with no intention of writing a song. This takes the pressure off of you having to create "that" sound for your particular song in progress, and allows you to just enjoy experimenting and tweaking sounds.

I also suggest you record all of your experimentation so you can cut up the good bits later. If you get in the habit of having sessions devoted to sound design, you will often find yourself inspired by some of the sounds you come up with, and ready to work them into a song.

This works very well because now the sounds are already there, and you can get to the business of writing songs and enjoying yourself with less technical interruptions.

The Most Important Habit You Can Ever Learn

What if I told you that if you could master just one habit, all the others would fall into place? How much further do you think you could get with your Music? How about the rest of your life?

Well there is one habit that is truly a magic bullet for all other habits. I don't say this lightly, because I don't believe in magic bullets in 99.9% of cases. Then again, most people think a magic bullet has to be easy. A one click solution.

Well this habit is certainly simple, but it's not easy. It will take work. But I promise you that if you can commit to thirty days of this habit, it will come naturally to you instead of being a struggle.

This "habit" is less of a habit and more of a habitual way of reacting. Let me explain.

If someone were to yell at you, hit you or cut you off on the freeway, you have a natural way of reacting. It's not really even something you think about. Your reaction has become a normal part of your personality. People can generally expect a certain response from you. Does this mean you are stuck in your ways? Most likely, yes... unless you make a conscious effort to change.

What you might not realize, is that there is a moment between an action and your reaction. (Don't worry, all of this is leading somewhere, I promise). If you can consciously pause before reacting to something, you have a small window of time in which to change your reaction. This is huge for you. This means you can take control of these reactionary habits.

Why changing a habit is so hard

We are creatures of habit. 80% (probably more) of what we do every day are habits that have been ingrained in us. We do them without even thinking. This is a good thing. This means that our brains can put its energy into processing new incoming data instead of having to concentrate on everything minute thing we do.

The downside to this, is that it's tough to change these automatic habits. Even when we do try to change, it's not uncommon to find ourselves going back to the old habit without even realizing it. But how did these habits form in the first place?

Every time we do a new task, we are building new pathways in the brain. The more we repeat the habit, the stronger the pathway. The stronger the pathways, the more automatic the habit.

From the same line of thinking, we can also conclude that as we stop doing a habit regularly, strong pathways become weaker and eventually die off.

So why is changing a habit so hard? Because you are not only creating a new pathway that is weak, but the habit you are changing is really strong. Understanding this makes all the difference in the world.

One habit to rule them all

As promised, I'm going to bring this all together for you now and give you the one habit that can improve your creative habits as well as every area of your life.

Stop worrying about the actual habits you are trying to adapt, because the habit itself is not the problem.

The real problem is and always has been your reaction to your new habits!

This is an extremely powerful thing to know. This means that as you change your reaction to new habits, *all* new habits become easier.

The "I don't feel like it" habit

Throughout your life, your brain's job is to keep you within your own version of the status quo. Once again, the reason for this is that your brain tries to reserve *thinking* energy as much as possible and prefers to run on autopilot. For that very reason, your brain will throw at you the "I don't feel like it" reaction to anything that requires *thinking* energy.

Kind of ironic that the brain doesn't particularly like to think huh?

So there you are, lying in bed and you realize you forgot to brush your teeth. You're warm, tired and you know *just one day* is not gonna kill you.

You are sitting at the computer knowing you should be working on your music but habitually when you feel like you *should* make music, your reaction is to check your email and post on Twitter and Facebook.

You look at your gut knowing that you should stop eating shitty food and get an exercise routine, but your usual reaction is cozying up to the couch and watching some mindless reality TV show while devouring a whole box of Hot Pockets.

This is the "I don't feel like it" habit, and you're letting it control your life. Want to do something about it yet?

A new reaction

You can't blame your brain for this. It's only following orders. However you react to thoughts, feelings and situations the most, become the brains *go to* response. You need to consciously build a new reaction to these thoughts.

Here are some techniques I use to generate a new reaction:

1. Search out the "*I don't feel like it*" virus by asking "What am I avoiding right now?" Every time you ask yourself this question, you'll certainly discover something you've been putting off. Whether it's doing dishes, making a call or finishing your new song, you'll be pointed directly to an immediate action step.

    What makes doing the right thing difficult is that because it's not an ingrained habit, it's simply not going to *feel* right. Sometimes it's going to feel all sorts of wrong. This is normal. Do it anyway. After a week, or sometimes less, it won't feel wrong anymore. After a month, it'll feel wrong to *not* take action.

2. Understand that *I don't feel like it* is only a thought you give meaning to. Most people let it mean they should not do something they know they should. What I do when I get that thought (which is usually when I'm warm in bed) is interpret the thought as a huge call to action and immediately jump out of bed and do what I don't feel like doing. I look at it as a message from my old self calling for my new self to come to the rescue. It's the old me desiring to become a better me.

3. I'll sometimes say to myself, "Let's get uncomfortable!" and not let it make me flinch. I laugh to myself at how I used to react to these feelings and what a wimp I was.

4. I'll journal for two full pages to see if I can uncover beliefs that are holding me back.

5. I'll make a daily *To Do* list breaking down intimidating projects or goals into bite sized tasks (thirty minutes to an hour). If I can do even one thing on the list each day, it's amazing how much I can accomplish without stress.

Commit

You'll never build these new pathways in your brain if you aren't practicing a new task every day. It doesn't have to be a long time spent but rather getting started on something every day, even if it's only ten or fifteen minutes. Commit to thirty days of becoming aware of your "I don't feel like it" response and you'll change your life massively.

I don't feel like making my bed or showering right now. Guess what I'm gonna do once I finish writing this?

How to Stop your Social Media Addiction

Social media, with all its benefits and new ways to connect has some serious downsides for creative people. I would never suggest that someone not use what is being offered as some of the best communication tools in history, but you have to come to terms with how this technology is rewiring the brain, and not always for the better.

How many times a day do you run the cycle of checking your email, then your twitter feed (first to see if you got any retweets, and then browse the timeline for anything interesting) followed by checking messages and notifications on Facebook and Google plus, then off to Flickr and Pinterest, just to make sure you aren't missing anything? And what do we do when the cycle is done? Check our email again, just to make sure nothing new has come in, thus starting an endless cycle.

Sound Familiar?

Recently I read an article in a magazine (can't recall which now) called *iCrazy*, and it discusses reports that social media, internet and gadget addiction is leading to some serious ADD, depression, anxiety and some pretty crazy behavior. Our brains are losing the ability to log off and if we let it continue unchecked, our devices will enslave us instead of free us.

I've decided to put some serious effort into curbing my internet habits in hopes of gaining more energy and motivation for more important things, like writing and making music. In doing this, I've made some pretty big discoveries that I'd like to share.

I've found that most of this cycle of addiction stems from one nasty habit and learning to eliminate it little by little can give you back your control over the technology.

The reaction

This drives almost everything we do on social media. We post, people react, and we get a shot of dopamine, the drug of choice for the masses.

How to be the best in the world

Being the best in the world at something is a pinnacle that so many reach for but so few ever obtain. Being number one isn't just a hair above number two. In fact, number one can command two to three times what number two commands, and up to ten times more than those below that.

I want *you* to be number one.

Have you ever given it much thought? Have you ever allowed yourself to think at that level? Why not? Don't think you'll ever be good enough? Do you think being the best means you have to sell your soul? Sell out?

I want to offer a different perspective that may change the way you look at art, and yourself as an artist.

What makes someone the best? Does everyone agree on who is the best in every category? I think not. In fact, some artists that we look at as the best, got very little attention, let alone admiration for their work, until they were long dead.

In other words, it's impossible to be the best artist or musician for all people at all times. It's too broad and there are too many people with different tastes.

When we start to break things down into smaller and smaller categories, it becomes much easier to agree on who is the best.

If you want to be the best in the world at something, you have to define who you are in very specific terms. Something that you can perfect and call your own. Sure you're going to be influenced by others, but like a great recipe, there is some twist that you do that makes it your very own and makes others choose your recipe instead of others. Maybe your unique flavor isn't for everyone. Neither is escargot. You can use this to your advantage. The less people who are attempting to do what you do, in the way you do it, the better.

The reason we don't have more world class artists, it that everyone is too busy trying to be a *second rate someone else* instead of the best *them* in the world!

You are the only thing that makes you unique. You are the one who will bring magic to what you do, if you start listening to your inner voice and give it time to develop. Stop jumping everybody else's train and create your own train that people will want to ride. Perfect it as you go. Put your 10,000 hours in and stay with *your* passion instead of somebody else's.

When you see a new genre of music blowing up and making people famous, realize that it's already too late to make a name for yourself doing what they do, the way they do it. Sure you'll get some quick attention for a bit, but you'll never be the best. The best is already taken.

When Brian Eno decided to make a type of music without drums and without much of a structure, people thought he was crazy and very few people followed him (in the beginning). But he stayed his path instead of being influenced by what was popular, or even what his fans expected of him. Now he is considered a master of ambient music (among many other talents he has developed). He created his own niche and he is considered the best in the world at what he does. It is now too late to be the best in the world at making ambient music, just like it's too late to be the best at dubstep or rock.

If you are going to be world class, you must find your own voice. There will never be another person on the planet who will ever be better at being you than you are. Being you is your legacy. Get off the follower's path and start leading your own path again.

Like every great artist before you, redefine what it means to be the best in the world.

Your potential. Are you reaching it?

I don't mean to get all "woo-woo" on you, but your creative potential is pretty unlimited.

Yes YOU!

So why aren't you where you want to be? What is it that is holding you back from completing that EP you've been planning to write? Why aren't you signing your tracks onto your favorite labels? Why aren't you playing some of the great gigs that are happening all year round, all around the world?

See, you are pure potential at every moment, but there is a huge difference between potential and making that potential your reality. Many of the things you do that you think are going to get you where you want to go are just increasing your potential energy. But that is not enough. It's like drawing back the string on your bow but never releasing the arrow.

Buying music books or magazines that you never read, is potential energy wasted. Reading them but not putting any of the things you've read into immediate action is even more wasted energy.

Watching tutorials without following along, just to cram more time into watching more videos is a waste of your time and energy.

Reading this book and not finding a way to put what you've learned into action is as much of a waste as "thinking about" giving that homeless guy $5 and instead walking by without even making eye contact. The "thought" might make you feel like a better person, just as much as reading about music production makes you "feel" smarter, but you are fooling yourself.

You are NOT the person you think you are until you put those potential thoughts into action. (You can tweet that, go ahead!)

I know this sounds pretty harsh, but it's important that I snap you out of your dream world and let you know that it's going to lead to nowhere unless you take some massive action toward your goals.

The beginning

Now that I have made you aware that you are wasting precious time and energy, you might be wondering what steps you can take to change this. Well, I am extremely pleased that you asked!

It's time to do the one thing us humans seem to have the hardest time doing....

Think for yourself

You've been spending so much of your time letting others think for you, that you've started thinking they are your own thoughts. In fact, as you read or watch new information you typically drop one approach for another. It's like a dog who drops the yellow ball in his mouth when he sees a red ball (I was going to say blue ball, but I thought that might throw us off topic).

When you are truly thinking for yourself, you need less information input. This is because instead of looking for others to tell you what to do, you are choosing a direction and moving. The only time you hunt information is when you are stuck and need a tip to get you unstuck. You do a quick google search, watch the video or read the post that suits your needs, and then you are back to work.

This is the path to potential energy, bursting into life.

But where do I start?

Although the better question to ask is usually "When do I start?" (Hint, it's *now*), I think this is a very valid question. Especially if you have several goals in mind.

You aren't going to be able to write an album, a book and start your career as a stand-up comedian all at the same time. That's like constantly changing the target you are aiming at, and never having time to lock on and pull the trigger on any one of them.

First you want to write down your several goals so you can see them. Understand that you have to get one goal off the ground before you can start on another. Once you are in the air, it'll be much easier to maintain, but it starts with tons of focus on one goal without distractions.

This means you will need to prioritize your goals.

I'll warn you now. Chasing money as your number one priority will not only kill your art, but will also kill your income. A person who only wants money and fame will have very little value to give the world. Everything you want in life will be in trade for the value you give to people. Everything comes through people, everything.

Often you'll find that accomplishing one goal will greatly assist you reaching your other goals, once the first goal is off the ground. For example, if you want to be both a DJ and producer, my greatest suggestion to you would be to take on Producing first. Nothing will raise your status faster and give promoters confidence that you can get asses into a club or venue more than a couple well respected tunes. It's like an instant resume. If people have heard of you, you'll have 50 times the opportunities than if you have no productions under your belt. Make sense?

Break it down

Big goals are a double edge sword. On one hand, a big dream will inspire you enough to push through great obstacles. On the other hand, they can seem extremely overwhelming to the point where you start reading tons of books and watching tons of videos that all give you different advice. Don't do that.

Once again, pull out a sheet of paper and break down your goal to doable actions. Each action should be a thirty minute to one hour task at most. If a task will take ten hours, break it down further into ten or twenty chunks. It might seem like breaking it down like that will make everything take forever. It won't. If you only worry about tackling a few "chunks" a day, you will reach your goals faster than you realize and without stress. When working toward your goal, keep an eye on the big picture, but put your focus completely on the now.

If you get stuck, give yourself fifteen to twenty minutes (tops) to learn only what you need to get to the next step. This way, all your time is devoted on taking action instead of just building potential that will never be used.

Mind map

Mind mapping is a simple way to see your plan of attack visually. It's like making an outline. What makes this important, is that you might find you left out an important step that you realize must go before what you are currently trying to take action on. This is going to happen. Your mind map will keep things organized as you figure things out. It also is like leaving breadcrumbs to follow if you ever need to take on a similar task again.

Here's a free mind mapping site. http://mind42.com/

If you prefer the outline format, I recommend Workflowy. https://workflowy.com/

80/20 - Your music production

For those not familiar with 80/20 principles, welcome to the principles that will give you your life back. I mean that quite literally.

The principle was suggested by management thinker Joseph M. Juran. It was named after the Italian economist Vilfredo Pareto, who observed that 80% of income in Italy was received by 20% of the Italian population. The assumption is that most of the results in any situation are determined by a small number of causes.

The concept of 80/20 has been around for a long time and we seem to be finding it's algorithm in pretty much everything that can be measured. It works in both macrocosms and microcosms.

In the grand scheme of things, 80% of everything you are doing right now is only getting you about 20% of the results. These are tasks that should be discarded to focus on the 2nd half of the rule. 20% of the things you are now doing are giving you 80% of your results. These are the things you want to do more of.

Let's look at some things in your life where 80/20 has a big effect.

- 20% of the things you eat give you 80% of the benefits
- 20% of your exercise routine gives you 80% of your results
- 20% of your workday creates 80% of your productivity

Get the idea?

So how can we take this kind of knowledge and apply it to music making?

I thought you'd never ask :-)

So let's look at some things that might be holding you back from being a more productive artist.

Not enough time

This is a huge obstacle for many aspiring producers and it has stopped many very talented people from ever getting to the starting line with their music career. Let's use the 80/20 principle and see if we can free up a large percentage of your time.

Let's look at some time-sucks that might be taking you away from making music. Remember, 80% of what you are doing is only attributing to 20% of the things you are getting done.

These things might fit in that category:

- Checking email or Social media more than a couple times a day.

- Phone calls that could be 80% shorter and still give you the same results

- Errands you might be running every day that you might be able to accomplish in 1 well planned trip per week

- Taking your least productive hour of the day (usually the last hour before you go to sleep) and adding that hour in the morning by getting up an hour earlier. This will give you a highly productive time before your day gets crazy (Thanks to Mike Monday for this one)

- Needless time spent stressed and worried over a future that will likely never happen

- How much of the TV you watch each week is largely garbage that does nothing to improve your life?

Are you getting the picture here? Apply the 80/20 principle to your time-sucks, and watch how time for music production magically opens up for you.

Music Production overwhelm

How much time do you spend trying to learn everything about making music while doing nothing with that knowledge?

It's like you had a tornado hit your creative brain and now you have all these tiny fragments of information, to do lists, tips, tricks and widely opposing opinions, so disorganized that you have zero idea where to start.

The truth is, 80% and maybe more of the crap you've filled your head with is just an addiction to consuming information. It's really just procrastination disguised as productivity. If you aren't going to put the information you are watching to use in the next 10 minutes, it's useless and a waste of your time and creative energy.

Between these scenarios, which do you think will give you 80% of your best results? 1 or 2?

1. Listening to 20 different people all telling you 20 different versions of the "right" way to get something done.

2. Trusting your own instincts and making a decision on your own, always evaluating and improving upon your own approach and only going outside yourself briefly to keep perspective.

1. Spending a week in forums trying to find out what the best possible synth or plugin to use. Buying and downloading all 50 of them and then searching tutorials to learn each one (just in case one synth might be ever slightly better at 1 or 2 things).

2. Giving yourself 1 hour to see what synths are out there, reading the "cliff notes" that matter to you and choosing 1 to learn in depth.

When starting a new song.....

1. Going through every synth, preset and sample until you find the drum sounds you are happy with, the right bass sound and all the additional elements.

2. Spending a day or 2 putting together a "go to" list of 10 or less sounds for each section that gives you quick access to sounds you already know you like.

If you've been choosing option 1 throughout your music production journey, welcome back to having a life!

Your turn

This is just the tip of a very large 80/20 iceberg (although 80% of that undiscovered iceberg probably isn't going to serve you any purpose). I challenge you to find other areas in your life that you can free up more of your mental energy for music making.

If you want to dive deeper into 80/20, I highly recommend looking up Perry Marshall. It takes a look at things from more of a business perspective, but is pretty easy to apply to almost anything.

The Suck Factor

I was talking to an artist I met and was intrigued that he was not only getting by with his art, but that he was living a pretty good life from it. Most of what he makes sells out pretty fast, and it's not like he lives in a big city, so I was impressed. Naturally, I had to investigate what made him tick and what separated him from all the starving artists.

I had already learned that he was very good at what he did, so I figured that he obviously was born with quite a gift.

Well... yes and no...

He definitely had a gift, but it wasn't as an artist. A least not from the start. His gift had more to do with his ability to plan for what most artists would consider red flags for any artistic pursuit. Sucking.

Where most people would try something once and fail, try again maybe a year or two later, fail again, then give up, he didn't look at things the same way. His art of choice was ceramics, something I tried once or twice and gave up (anyone need an ashtray?). What really surprised me is the story he told me and how he viewed his experience. It's not the way most of us approach things or define the experience at all.

Apparently, this artist was far from naturally gifted at ceramics. I guess he started off as a hell of an ashtray sculptor himself, but he came from a physics background and instead of feeling like a failure, he looked at his artistic venture in a more scientific way. If one approach didn't work, he would take note and try again slowly improving his technique. Sometimes it would take ten or twenty tries just to figure out where the issue in the process was. It seemed that in his mind, he already knew he would nail it given enough time. Keep in mind that he wasn't even thinking yet about selling or even showing his work. He was still getting the process down.

After about 1000 attempts he was prepared to show his work, and people bought it up right away. Some things obviously sold better than others. There was also pricing to keep in mind. He didn't want a $20 piece to devalue his $500 pieces but he knew he needed both to make a good living. He didn't really have an artistic conflict about one thing selling better than another, because he simply enjoyed the process of creating, not necessarily the specific piece. He knew that his art was a job, a job he could love, but a job nonetheless.

This really hit me hard and made me take a good look at my creative beliefs, my work ethic and my definition of failure and success. Was I willing to try something ten times? 100? 1000 times? Until I had mastered my creative art? If I am being honest, I'd have to say no, and the reason for that is that I was defining failure as a certain number of times I don't succeed. Sound familiar?

Remember, there is a huge difference between the art you make and the art you share. Don't let the art you are making now deter you. If your goal is to be great at something, plan for a lot of sucking and missing the mark. Try not to let it get you down.

Remember that many people have to go to college for four to eight years before they are prepared to do what they do well. Can you imagine someone judging their architecture skills on what they were able to accomplish and understand after a week of schooling? So why then would we judge ourselves on our art or music before we put in the proper amount of time? From that point of view it sounds a bit silly doesn't it?

Now, once you become a "natural" at one aspect of music, don't think you weren't meant to explore another style just because your work is not nearly up to par with the style you excel at. How about making 100 attempts at it before you judge?

I can give you a perfect example for myself in how I will use this new process. I am not great with many soft synths. My strengths would be Ableton's Operator, Reason's Subtractor, and TAL's Juno 106 clone. With most soft synths I just poke around on the pre-sets, tweak the knobs I understand, and then use EQ, Filter and FX to get an interesting sound. If I don't get the sound I'm looking for, I go back to the familiar. This, I must admit, slows me down and limits my options.

You could argue that less options is a good thing and I would strongly agree, however I believe that too many options mainly becomes a problem if you are not already skilled or familiar with the tools you are using. For example, you can't have too many words in your vocabulary unless you have no idea what the words mean and how to use them in a conversation.

What I suggest you do to get better at more synths is take a week (or a month) on one new soft synth until you can consider myself proficient at it. Then you can add it as another option. I predict that doing this process a couple times will make the process go a bit faster each time as you find similarities and common themes among different tools.

- What is it that you think you are a failure at?

- Do you think you will still be a failure after 100 or more attempts?

- Are you willing to let go of instant gratification to allow yourself to improve at whatever pace is necessary?

If the art you make doesn't satisfy you, pat yourself on the back for the improvements you made since your last attempt, and then refocus on perfecting your weaknesses in your next attempt. When you attempt something new, set aside some time for the "suck factor".

Maybe that's why they call it suck-cess!

The takeaway

To wrap things up, here are some thoughts you should take away from this

- The more music you make, the better the quality will become.
- The more music you finish, the easier finishing music will become.
- Everybody struggles to sound good when they start
- The faster you make decisions, the less chance you have of getting stuck or having writer's block.
- The more decisions you make, the better your decision making instincts will become
- We will always aim for quality, whether we make it a conscious goal or not.
- You're only ever competing with yourself. Only aim to be better than you were yesterday.
- Quantity becomes quality over time.

Committing to your music

So let's be honest.

How many of you make a commitment to something creative only to find it in the shitter within weeks?

All of us have likely failed, or have dropped the ball on our goals.

Why is this?

Try to think about any positive habit that you have been able to perform for a full thirty days without missing a single day. I have attempted this many times, but have succeeded very few. It takes serious mental effort to stick with something until it becomes second nature.

Your first challenge to overcome is just how wrong it feels to break your daily habits. Even if you're wasting your time with mindless TV or browsing the internet, to do something else during that time is difficult, especially if it's creative. I seriously would start thinking about doing dishes, cleaning the bathroom or laundry, just to avoid the risk of sucking at my creative endeavors.

The "November" Challenge

One November, my girlfriend and I challenged ourselves to eating a strict Paleo diet up until Thanksgiving. I'm proud to say it was a success, which felt really good to achieve. As often happens, one success can create the momentum you need for another.

So with that in mind I felt more confident in taking on a creative challenge, but before I dove right in, I bought a book that had apparently helped writers a lot and I read it front to back in a day. It's called The War of Art by Steven Pressfield. This put a serious fire under my ass and made me as ready as I was gonna get.

The December (and beyond) experiment

Starting the following month on December 2nd, I started an experiment as much for myself as it was for other music producers. This experiment was to challenge myself as well as all my readers to produce music for at least one hour a day, every day for as long as they could go. Each day they were to make a simple post sharing a snippet of the work they'd done that day with the group, and give us a brief description of their process for that day.

In the first few days of starting this, I got a bunch of "I'm so in!", "Let's do this!", and "Count me in" comments. Many of which never posted any of their work. Several put in the effort for a few days and then fell into obscurity. Still others did their best to stay in the game, even though they missed a day here or there.

To get an idea of the commitment level people have in general, I tracked the first 36 days. I counted a day for either posting a song, or commenting on what they completed that day. In that amount of time, here is how participation of Facebook broke down:

85 people "liked" the post, 7 people "shared" the post and 50 people commented.

Of those 50 people:

- I made music 35 days (missed one day - Dec 26th)
- 1 person made music 29 days
- 1 person made music 25 days
- 1 person made music 15 days
- 1 person made music 7 days
- 2 people made music 6 days
- 2 people made music four days
- 3 people made music three days
- 4 people made music twice
- 11 people made music once
- 23 people didn't post any music.

As expected, the number of people who publicly committed vs those who followed through is pretty small. The lower the number of days producing, the higher the number of people. None of us produced for the full 36 days.

For me, this experiment proved that committing to daily work on music not only increases your musical output, but it also improves the quality of your music. You truly do get better, and although the process is never simple, it gets enormously easier the more you do it (typically after 30-45 days).

It seems that repetition of a skill is necessary for improvement. It's like pushing a rock up a mountain. When you stop the upward motion it's going to slip back downhill, and you'll likely have to rediscover that skill from the beginning again.

I can testify to this myself. In the past, I would write sporadically and then go through a huge time of being unmotivated or uninspired. The longer I stayed away, the harder it was to start again. I would stare at the screen not knowing where or how to begin. Sure, some creative instincts stay with you, but since they haven't been regularly exercised, you won't be on your game.

In those 36 days, I personally finished 7 songs. I had *never* finished this much music before, and I've also been very happy with the results. My goal for past years used to be to finish just 1 song a month, 12 a year. When I would fail at that, I'd go for 6 a year. In actuality, I'd usually finish 2 or 3 songs, one usually being a remix; and if I'm honest now, every song was a struggle, with long periods of not having much fun.

The daily approach has put the fun back into the whole process!

Of course there will days that you don't feel like working on music, but not making music won't even be an option. You'll have too many fresh ideas to get to & too much momentum. Don't worry if a tune you are working on doesn't come out amazing. Just put in your best effort, call it done and immediately jump on to the next song. When you are this productive, you become less worried about having a bum day, or making a tune that isn't a perfect ten.

It's much different when you are only making one song every few months. Each song matters so much, that the results can make or break your confidence in a big way. These days, my goal is more about beating resistance and procrastination. The rest just takes care of itself.

Your whole year might suck, unless...

A word about resolutions. You know, those usually useless commitments we make to our friends on a drunken New Years' Eve? Or when you wake up one morning and think "F**k it! This shit's gonna change!"

And here we are. A clean slate. A fresh start. A chance to start anew. This isn't the first time though and it also won't likely be the last.

- What were your goals and resolutions last time?

- How did your reality stack up with your intentions?

- Did you over achieve or under achieve?

My guess is that most of you probably fall in the area of accomplishing less than 25% of what you had intended.

Did your goals to really dive into your music and crank out some tunes or play more DJ gigs get side tracked by "life"? How many months in the year before you just went back to your old ways?

It's a lot like people who make a resolution to get into shape, but stop going to the gym two or three months later. The intentions are high, but the results end up staying mostly the same.

Broadcasting

How many of you broadcast your goals publicly? If you don't, why not? Is there something in your brain that already thinks you won't succeed? I can't even begin to tell you your chances of failure if you hide in the shadows and stay on the sidelines with your goals. Broadcasting your goals is an exercise in stepping out of your comfort zone, and having the public hold you accountable. Even better if you join a group or forum with likeminded people with similar goals.

Your habits don't change, unless...

No matter how hard you try, year after year, your habits probably won't change if you are taking the same approach that you have been taking in the past. This is because you get fired up in the beginning and the new habit seems easy for a week or two, but then reality sets in and the honeymoon is over. You *really* want to take a night off. It won't hurt, right?

Yes, it does. *Bigtime!*

See, forming a habit isn't all about feeling great about doing the new habit. This simply won't happen. You're going to go through a phase of hating the new habit, whether it be flossing, exercising, eating healthier or finally kicking out some great tunes. It's all the same stuff. A habit is a habit.

Thirty Days or nothing

If you can't get yourself to do a new habit for thirty days straight, the habit simply won't stick. This is because the habit you are really trying to form, isn't the habit itself, but the habit of doing it anyway, even when you don't feel like it. If you think it's possible to form a new habit without thinking it won't suck sometimes, you're delusional. There are, however, ways to make this thirty day process easier.

- One habit at a time - Unfortunately for most people, they set themselves up to fail, by wanting to change more than 1 thing at a time. Every failure in accomplishing these things is just sending a message to your brain that you are a failure, and not capable of changing. Don't set yourself up like this. How about going for four goals for the whole year? One goal every three months. This is extremely important, because one change is easy for your brain to take on, and each success builds greater strength for the next goal.

- Bite sized habit forming - Let's say you want to finish more songs in the New Year. Can you just do ten minutes a day at the same time every day for thirty days? Can you accomplish that ten minutes of real work, even if you don't feel like it? Can you push aside all the excuses? If you can do this for thirty days straight, you will have formed a habit that you can expand on, and slowly build up to twenty minutes, thirty minutes, and on to an hour a day. Once you've pushed past the resistance enough times, it will become second nature to go right to the task, even when you don't feel like it. What many people don't realize, is that *most of the resistance goes away the moment you get started*.

- Breaking down big tasks - Do your goals seem too big for you? Don't give up on them. Simply break the big goal down to a bunch of thirty minute tasks, or even less if you want. Instead of spending hours at your desk feeling overwhelmed every day, how about accomplishing two thirty minutes tasks a day? This is how I accomplish most of my big projects. If I didn't approach things this way, I'd never complete anything.

- Stop preparing to do work - Cleaning your desk or listening to a music loop you created for hours on end, researching or watching tutorials is NOT working. Find another time to prepare for work. When you sit down for your ten minutes, or thirty minutes or whatever it is, *do actual work*! If you get stuck after your initial work session, set a timer to research what you need and then get back to work. Don't get dragged into YouTube comments or social media bullshit. You're not missing anything. It'll all be there when you're done. The only difference is that you will be one of the few people posting on Facebook that has actually accomplished something to be proud of for the day, instead of dicking around on the internet.

Attach a new habit to a current habit

The best way to get a new habit ingrained is to attach it to another daily habit. You can make this current habit a trigger for the new habit. Let's say you have a cup of tea every day at 2 PM. This is perfect. So start your new habit directly after your tea, every day at the same time. You'll be amazed how often after that cup of tea your brain will go "Ok, time to sit down at the studio". Once you get past the resistance, it will become second nature, and you'll wonder what the big deal was about in the first place.

Stay off the sidelines

Most people who try something new usually do it as privately as possible. This bums me out because they are missing the most important part of learning, and that is tapping into the "mastermind". Hundreds or thousands of brains working together to problem solve, support, focus, collaborate and hold each other accountable. No man is an island. Get off the sidelines.

Stop devouring, start applying

- "Just one more tutorial"

- "Once I learn how to get that sound, I'll be set"

But it's never just one more tutorial, and it's never just one more sound, is it?

Stop devouring information and start applying what you are learning. What is the point of reading a dictionary start to finish before sending an email, in the event that you might be at a loss of the right word at a certain point? Doesn't that seem kinda stupid? Doesn't it make more sense to have a dictionary handy for when you get stuck on a word or spelling? Same with making music, or any other habit. Use your brain, push it to the limits with your own problem solving. Show a little fucking confidence, instead of always having to see how everybody else is doing things. A new technique not immediately applied is no way to build confidence. It's just compounding the fact that you have no confidence because you have nothing original to say.

Harsh, yes, but I want you to know the truth so you don't screw up another year. It disappoints me what people do with a clean slate. Why not instead, keep the slate clean by taking on one task at a time until completion? This essentially cleans your slate over and over throughout the year. Don't you think that would make for a more inspiring, focused and less stressful year? Can you imagine how much more you can easily get done year after year?

Mindset

The beauty of not getting the sound you want

How long have you spent in the past agonizing over trying to get *that* sound?

Trying to get the exact sound in your head and succeeding can be very satisfying, but it's largely a waste of time. Let me explain further.

That sound in your head that you are trying to put into your song most likely came from another song by another artist. Now I'm not against sampling, borrowing or even downright stealing when it seems appropriate, but I think you're missing out on a whole lot of sound opportunities when you get locked onto a specific sound in your head.

Having a basic concept is one thing, but when you block out every alternative to the particular sound, you are also filtering out many more unique and original sounds. I've been there many times myself. You are so focused on *that* sound, you don't even recognize when you are creating genius in the moment.

A much better approach is to start with a basic idea and then let it go once you get started. Let yourself be guided in the moment. This will still require some focus so you don't go way off the trail, but even that can be a worthwhile journey.

When your music takes you somewhere you hadn't expected, you become both the driver and the passenger. This is the best place for an artist to be.

When I find myself inspired by a song or artist (which happens quite a bit), I consciously try to avoid thinking in terms of bass tone, drums rhythm etc., especially if it's already a song that is in the same genre that I make. Instead, I think of words to describe the vibe or tone of the song. I might use abstract words to describe different elements like "*cotton candy pads*" or "*underwater bass that periodically comes up for air*". Or maybe I'll think of the song as a story "*Lonely satellite dreaming of leaving its orbit to explore the universe and perhaps interact with other intelligent machines*".

Once I've done this, I'll usually put it away for a week or so. Long enough to forget the songs that inspired those descriptions. When you return to these descriptions, your brain can explore its own unique way of expressing these images, with only a subtle nudge from the original influence.

I think this is also why coming back to unfinished songs months later can often sound more inspiring to you (not that I suggest not completing a song unless you've truly put in your best effort). You forget that place you were trying to get to and become free to take it in a new direction. You no longer think of the sound you failed to create, but hear it for what it is. When you have no particular path in your head to follow, forging your own path becomes the only option. We are still in the business of finishing songs after all. You just want those songs to sound like you and not a Xerox copy of your influences.

In the case of music making, you should be thankful when you don't get the sound you want, because once you let that go, you can explore what inspires you in the moment. Whole new genres of music were born this very way, so embrace it and know you are helping music evolve.

How to beat the competition and build a fan base

If you've been producing for a while or even if you're just getting started, you might have realized that there are a *lot* of producers out there releasing music. This obviously makes for a pretty noisy environment out there when you are trying to get noticed yourself.

You know that if you had the audience that some of these veterans had, you'd be making bigger sales and getting all the great gigs too. It seems like everywhere you turn, someone you know is releasing tunes on Beatport, Amazon or one of the other digital outlets for artists, and let's be honest, some of it is really good.

Then there are those giving away their music for free. With all this going on, getting noticed and making some small living from your music seems like a distant concept that now feels largely obsolete. Well, that is definitely one way to look at it but it's not going to help you at all with your goals.

The way to get noticed is largely the same as it was in the past. You can't look at the other producer's audience with envy.

Do you think all those admirers came out of nowhere? Do you think they were just handed this fan base?

Nope, they had to earn each and every one. Of course getting your first 1000 fans will always be harder than the next 10,000 and so on.

There is no competition

Ok, yes, you are competing for attention, just like everyone else. Luckily, most of the major attention platforms are free. That of course is great news and bad news. When everyone can promote themselves for free, no one stands out, right?

Well, I don't know about that.

When I am out at a club with 1000 or more people, many people fade into the background, but then again some people stand out more than others. Some people seem to have something the others don't that grabs your attention. These days you have to get really clear about that *something* or you'll get nowhere fast.

People aren't buying your music anymore. They are buying *you*.

You are the thing that needs to shine. Your personality is going to draw people in or repel them. Having a personality that people are able to connect with and having decent music will likely get you much further than having great music but no personality for people to interact and relate to.

If you make yourself public and share more of who you are, people will be more interested in anything you produce, whether it be music, art, books or anything else you can create.

Don't envy the big guy

When I was younger I was in a band that wanted to be the next *Depeche Mode* or *The Cure*. We felt that if we were put in front of their crowd, we would sell a lot of records and a lot of tickets. We also knew that wasn't possible. Instead we had to make a noise from scratch and develop a fan base one at a time.

Our strategy was to look good and go out as a group just having fun and meeting people. We *always* had flyers with us, whether we were at a nightclub, a party, or out at a restaurant. If we saw someone that looked cool, we would introduce ourselves, maybe have a quick chat and leave them with a flyer to remember us by.

With this method we grew from playing our first gig to fifteen people (mostly family) at a dumpy club called the Green Door, to selling out The Roxy in Hollywood within about a year. It turns out, when you build your own tribe, instead of trying to put yourself in front of someone else's tribe, there isn't nearly the amount of noise, and people will be more inclined to give you their attention and tell others about you.

Once you have built a real fan base of people who are not just sold on your music, but on the people behind it (no, not Facebook likes, but people who will actually go to your shows and buy your music), many of the shortcuts that the bigger artists always seem to get will start showing up for you as well. The thing we understood is that we had do small in a big way.

A lot of producers don't have the right work ethic, and some assume that you either get lucky or you don't. In the real world, luck only happens for a very few number of people. The percentage is so small as to not be worth aiming for. Instead make your own luck.

If we keep with the Hollywood theme to fame, *Motley Crue* and *Guns and Roses* started that same way. Getting 100 people to their first few shows and growing from there. Obviously, once you have the attention of the people, you have to show them you are deserving of it.

I think a combination of great music and a strong personality helps. Make sure you actually put the work in where it counts. In the online world you don't gain fans by spamming people to death. It's not very rock n roll to use such desperate measures like that.

You don't want to just send people to Beatport to find you. It's like someone trying to pick you out from a crowd of 50,000 people. Even if they *do* find you, it's a very impersonal experience.

You're much better starting people off on your Facebook fan page (since this is where so many people congregate), then as you build relationships and trust, you can invite people to your Soundcloud or Bandcamp page, which allows you to create a more personal experience with your music. You can get even more intimate with Google Hangouts, your website and other places where they can be in your environment and catch your vibe.

In business marketing there is something known as the "Funnel". This is where you lead a customer to the sale in a certain way so as to not lose their interest or scare them off. The better the funnel, the better chance to get people to invest in you happily, while telling their friends how great you are in the process.

This is because you gave value in a comfortable environment before you asked them to invest their time or money. In the eyes of the general public these days, you start off at a disadvantage.

They most likely are in the frame of mind that "Your band probably sucks and isn't worth the time to even click on a free link".

This is why the "funnel" is so important. You need to have a plan for how to lead people to buying your albums and coming to your shows without looking like a used car salesman. It's not about the sale, it's about the relationship.

If you use Facebook, Twitter, YouTube and Google as examples, you were lead to their sites because they were free and offered something of value without asking anything in return. They all learned that the longer they could sustain a free model, the bigger the trust in the relationship becomes.

In the case of the musician, this can be sneak peeks at songs in progress, the artwork, behind the scenes jam sessions, blogging, sharing pictures and even sharing some of your music free.

If you look at the model used by Trent Reznor and wife Mariqueen with *How to Destroy Angels*, they gave their first four song EP away for free, and these weren't some throwaway songs, it was great stuff. Now when they release something new, the sales come rushing in.

I know that might be a bad example because of Trent's iconic reputation, but it shows that even the big guys understand the power of this model. The longer you can sustain this, the more likely they are to act when you ask for their support. You've earned it and have built a relationship.

Ask someone you haven't built a relationship with for $5 and you're a bum. Ask a good friend and he'll insist you take $10.

Stop listening, START SHOUTING

All of us who make music, want it to reach an audience. The goal is to reach the largest audience possible while keeping our creative integrity. While we have the greatest opportunity in history to reach an audience quickly, there is a flip side of the equation that is making it more difficult in this day and age.

Attention

More than any other time in history, our attention is spread incredibly thin. The power to get attention is now in everybody's hands but most of us are really bad at it. We have a hard time managing our own attention let alone that of others. Everyone is throwing art and opinions in each other's face on a never ending basis. Some of it might be good, but when people are bombarded with so much of it, even the good stuff fades into the background.

Playing it safe

In an attempt to get people's attention, artists and musicians have traded their creative individualism to become marketers. Unfortunately not the good kind. They do research, trying to find out what people are already buying and then put their creative focus on delivering *that* in an attempt to 'cash in'. From a business standpoint this can work, sometimes really well, but from an artistic point of view, this is suicide.

Artists are not meant to survey their audience to find out what they want.

No *no* NO!

We tell *them* what they want! We do it loud and we do it proud!

Artistry is about changing the way people view the world and making your mark, not about conforming to the world as it currently is. Art is meant to move society forward, to show them the way, to carve out a new path. A great artist doesn't give a damn what you think and they shouldn't. They know more about art than their audience. This is why they have an audience in the first place!

The consumer

The consumer is constantly screaming "Give me what I want!", while inside they are really thinking "Inspire me", even if they aren't consciously aware of it. To give the customer what they want is everything that is wrong with music today. Popular music just continues to get more and more dumbed down. The consumer doesn't know what they want, plain and simple, and if you ask them, they will likely regurgitate something that has already been recycled, filtered, over produced and watered down for the masses.

Why is so much popular music watered down?

Plain and simple, it's safe. It doesn't offend people (except the minority that wants to turn things upside down). It's middle ground music that has appealed to the masses in the past, but is now wearing a different colored t-shirt to appear new.

If you listen to your audience, you are going to fall into mediocre, middle ground music that people love to ignore, while it plays in the background like a buzzing refrigerator (which can often make a much more beautiful sound than what is currently on the radio).

Make your mark

If you want to make a mark on the music scene, fitting in is the best way to disappear. There is just too much 'decent' music that all sounds similar. Why would anyone care about more of the same? You are just one of millions of people trying to sell or give away your music.

Although we all love music, there is just too much to consume. It's being thrown at us from every direction. Why would I stop and listen to *you*, especially if it's just the same-'ole stuff?

Take a look at the best bands throughout the ages. Which ones really stand out? Are they the safe, middle of the road bands, or the ones with a huge *"Fuck you!"* stamped on their forehead?

The ones that bent and broke the rules. The ones that spoke from their soul. The ones that were an assault on what we previously thought music could be. The ones that shouldn't have made it, but somehow were too good to ignore.

They were unapologetically themselves. If you are unapologetically pop because that is where the art in you takes *you*, then in my eyes you are still a rebel. Erasure is unapologetically pop and they are brilliant! This is because they know who they are, and they don't listen to what anybody says or survey where the market is going. They just do what they love.

This isn't the fucking stock market, people. If you are only looking for a quick cash cow, *don't make art*. Get into banking instead.

One of these is not like the others

My goal for you is that your creative voice gets so loud that it drowns out the chatter of the masses. Stop listening to opinion of others and start your own journey. When you are different, you attract the attention of people who care about art in music. When you are not like the others, you interrupt peoples' brains because you've just given them something unexpected that they don't yet have a clear definition of how to categorize. They have to stop and think, instead of the automatic "define and file away" pattern. Sure, this might not lead to sales in the millions, but if you consider the successes that came before you, that have stood the test of time, it's a damn good strategy! Plus, you maintain your artistic dignity, and that has to count for something.

What can you do today to become more like you *and less like them?*

Getting out of your own way

Whether it be music or another aspect of your life, at some point you've probably had someone respond to one of your concerns by suggesting that you just "get out of your own way" and everything will work out. Great advice right? Well, unfortunately, in most cases, neither the one delivering the message or receiving it really understand what the hell that even means.

"How am I supposed to get out of my own way?"

"This all sounds fine and dandy as some fancy statement to throw around, but how would I even apply this in practical terms?"

I'm glad you asked.

In truth, getting out of your own way is something you do quite a bit already and it helps much of your life flow far more easily. It makes very complex things we do effortless, but if we get in the way of these effortless actions, you will find the simplest things far more difficult.

To get deeper into this it's important that you look at what is going on in your mind and body when you are stressed or nervous vs. when you are relaxed and in the flow.

Can you describe the differences mentally and physically between the two? Do you feel this gets you any closer to understanding what it means to get out of your own way?

Let me drop you a hint:

Notice how naturally you act and how relaxed you are when you are around your close friends. You walk, talk and breathe freely, are focused on the moment, and only concerned with the good time you're having. The night flows without a hitch and your body and mind don't let you down.

Now let's put you in front of a pretty girl that you would really like to get to know (reverse this scenario if you are a straight female). What happens? You're thinking about what to do with your hands, making sure to keep eye contact but not to stare, hoping to hell she didn't catch you looking at her breasts. You try to speak but your mouth and voice seem to fail you. You stutter and fumble your words. You concentrate on if you are holding yourself confidently and relaxed. Your hands are sweaty, and basically, this first impression is a crash and burn.

What exactly was happening? Why did the simple things suddenly become so complex?

You were talking to yourself, judging every body movement, second guessing. This inner voice is making you so aware of every sensation you are experiencing and every potential way you can do things incorrectly, that suddenly doing things the correct way feels like a one in a million long shot.

Does this sounds familiar in other areas of your life? Music perhaps? I thought so.

See, the problem is, we rely on the opinions of this inner voice at the absolute worst times to seek its guidance. You didn't need guidance with your night out with your friends and that went fantastic. Your creative ventures need to become more like a night out with buddies, instead of an awkward night with a person you are trying to impress.

Yoda was right, there is no try.

If you want to better apply this skill (and yes, it is a skill) of getting out of your own way, you need to stop over preparing for genius and just have fun. I promise that your most inspired performances are going to happen when you aren't even trying. Sure, there will be a time and place to look at what you created objectively, but you will always need to distinguish between the voice that pushes you forward, and the one that holds you back from your potential.

Imagine if the solution to entering the genius level of music creation was simply your ability to ignore the noise of the mind and instead create for reasons beyond explanation. Imagine that all the tools you need are already in your hands and that magic doesn't come from the instrument, but from you. Your ability to look around at the tools you already have and have fun with them, is where the magic in you will start to be released.

Exploring new tools should never come from the thought process that you don't have enough already, but from a "this looks like something fun to explore" standpoint. If you aren't using what you already have to satisfy your obsession to create, you aren't being an artist. This is what sets us apart as artists, and it's the key to unlocking your potential.

Stop searching and second guessing. Start trusting and believing. Genius will soon follow.

Put your Brain to work

Your brain is a powerful thing. You hear this all the time but you forget just how amazing it is. Everything that has ever been accomplished has started as an idea or a problem to solve in the brain. Before I go off on a complete tangent I wanted to share some new ideas to boost your creativity.

I was talking to a friend who was awaiting confirmation on a release of one of his tracks on Richie Hawtin's Minus label (Now signed). We've talked a few times about our approaches to music and productivity in general and we tend to both shy away from getting overly technical. Instead we discussed training your brain for creativity, and finishing what we've started as two of the most important skills to develop.

This friend of mine had zero equipment besides his Mac. No outboard gear, no controllers. Just Ableton Live, Operator, one or two other synths, and his brain. Imagine that, a guy with minimal equipment making minimal music! This proves that you could make and release quality music without having to buy all kinds of equipment, but that's another story...

So instead of talking about how he makes his songs specifically, I want to share with you his creative approach. He is already a successful guy in a non-music industry, so he uses his idea generating and problem solving skills from one industry to the next. Ever notice that some people are successful in most everything they touch? I think there is something to the way these people think.

This is the simple approach.

- Have a notepad and recorder with you at *all* times. For many of us, we have this all in our iPhone. When you make an intention to record your ideas, your brain tends to give you more ideas. The more you take notes, write down lyric ideas, mixing and structuring ideas or melodies, the more your brain will feed you. I tend to use iPhone's notepad and email the note to myself. I use an app called Record for all my melodic and rhythmic ideas as well as field recordings. I also keep a notepad available to write things down. Usually when I'm making lists. It doesn't really matter what you use. It's more important to just try it, you'll be pleasantly surprised!

- Treat your brain like a well-respected and trusted employee. Your brain is really only limited to what you feel it's capable of. Put it to the test. My approach is to throw a creative or technical problem at it to solve before you go to sleep. You'll be surprised how often you come up with solutions by morning or within a couple days. I'd suggest starting small, just so you build a bit of confidence but once you get the hang of it, you can give it bigger and bigger tasks. Before you go to sleep, create a picture in your mind of the problem you're facing already solved and then let it go. When you sleep, you tap into some serious resources that simply aren't available in your waking life.

- Dream Log: Although this is completely unnecessary, I do my best to remember and write down my dreams, even if they seem irrelevant. The reason I do this, is that it trains your brain to tap into your dream state resources while you're awake. I think that is the point where fresh new ideas flow the best.

Put these ideas to use right away & witness the results!

Do happy people make crappy music?

Do drugs make you more creative?

This is one of those things that most artists have asked themselves or perhaps discussed with other artists over a couple drinks. I gave this a month to stir around my head before I attempted to write about it. I've always wanted to make music that mattered in one way or another yet at the same time wanted happiness, health, great relationships etc. I had this great fear that if I gave up all my bad habits and focused on the good in my life, my music would suffer. The question really comes down to this...

Do miserable or messed up people make great art? And if so, why?

I'll admit that I've had times of depression that lead to a wealth of powerful material. I've also had creative juices come when I was drunk or on drugs. Then again I'm sure everyone has had sober spurts of creativity in the shower or sitting on the toilet.

So what gives?

Here are my personal thoughts...

The wakeful mind is often more analytical and less creative. The sober mind tends to have a greater fear of being judged, so we prefer to fill our time with things that wouldn't highlight our lack of talent or skills. We are basically afraid to suck. It's much easier to convince yourself that you are far too busy to explore the genius that you really are (or rather the genius you would like others to believe you are). Better to stay quiet and be thought of as talented, than to open your mouth and prove the opposite.

These are some of the thoughts that creep in when the sober and generally happy mind starts a new project:

- Of all of my ideas, which idea is the best one?

- Are any of my ideas worth pursuing?

- What if I find out that my favorite idea sucks?

- What if I am technically not skilled enough to get my ideas out properly?

- Do I really have time in my life to pursue this creative avenue without sacrificing another part of my otherwise happy life?

- Is this music thing really the most mature thing for me to pursue?

Where do these thoughts come from? Unfortunately your inner critic speaks pretty loud when you want to try something new or challenging. Try sitting sober and doing nothing for fifteen minutes. No eating, no TV, no internet, no video games. Notice how you feel and what your mind is doing. Without distractions your mind is most likely restless and looking for distractions. See, what most of us call happy could more likely be defined as distracted. If you had the confidence, more often than not, this restlessness could be channeled into some great enjoyable work, but then you would have to shut off that inner voice.

Unfortunately many of us need to get out of our normal headspace to feel relaxed. That's probably why mood altering substances lend themselves to creativity, as does showering, or those moments before you fall asleep. These are all times that the mind relaxes a bit and also allows itself to wander. Many times the awake, sober mind doesn't look at daydreaming to be a very productive use of your time. Your mind usually tries to fill every moment it can with a distraction, and rarely leaves the open space that allows real creativity to shine.

That gets us through the productivity part, but what about the quality of your work when drunk, drugged out, stressed or depressed vs happy and sober.

I think this comes down to the intensity of your life experiences. The reason why content and generally happy people aren't creating their best work is because their happiness is rarely a peak experience, but rather just absence of bad events and emotions.

It's like the difference between reading words, and actually getting "lost" in a book. Which mindset would you expect to give you a better creative output? Life usually has to shake you up a bit in a positive or negative way to inspire you creatively because peak experiences knock you out of your "daily life" thoughts and force you to "let go" for a moment, or rethink something you thought you had figured out.

I have read (and tend to believe) that genius comes at moments when the brain is not actually thinking. Some people call this the "gap". Everyone has likely felt this unintentionally at one point or another, but it's difficult to create it "on demand". Personally, I've experienced this while driving or right before I fall asleep (if I can catch that moment), or when I wake up in the middle of the night remembering a dream or thought process. I've also had some great moments during meditation.

Einstein was known to give himself plenty of daydreaming time. Thomas Edison was able to create these moments on demand by falling asleep in a chair with a spoon in his hand and a pan at his feet. When he would start to doze off, the spoon would fall from his hand onto the pan and wake him up. At those moments he would get his great ideas. Many songwriters and artists will keep a pen and paper next to their bed, or a small recorder, with the intention of getting the ideas out when they come to mind.

The real answer is that it is much harder to produce a creative moment from scratch. Drugs, alcohol and extreme life circumstances are a shortcut that may be helpful in the beginning, but will eventually make you unable to enjoy your own creative success...or your life for that matter. Once these things become habits, they will no longer create peak experiences, and you'll just constantly be looking for something more (one big reason why you always want to buy a new piece of gear or software).

I think everything has it's time and place, but when you are no longer exploring new experiences and instead just repeating a pattern, the mind will no longer reward you with good ideas. Unless you can continue to get "lost" in your work, your thoughts will constantly be jumping back to every day concerns, and away from creative thinking.

Another reason you may lack productivity is that most of us are creatively lazy and unorganized. It's not like we don't have ideas, but they just stack up like a load of dirty dishes, until we have so many ideas that we don't know where to start. Many great ideas jump in our head but we don't take them seriously enough to write them down or record them right away. This is how most or our great ideas are lost. At the time we think the idea is so simple that we won't forget it, but within an hour we realize that charmingly simple idea is gone and you can't retrace it.

The best advice I can give you is to consistently try to have new experiences by visiting new places, trying new foods, taking on a new habit, meeting new people etc. I also recommend that you engulf yourself in other artists or musicians that excite you. I find some amazing stuff on YouTube that gives me new creative ideas. Although I make tutorial videos, I also constantly allow myself to be a student. I read blogs, books and short stories as well. I love when a new idea forces me to throw out old concepts. This is where new ideas can be created. Another idea is to create restrictive rules for yourself like:

- Only one synth for a whole song

- No chords, only melodies

- How long can you sustain one note in a song without it getting boring?

- How long can you sustain silence?

When your mind is given a new challenge, it thinks about the process differently and more creatively. Your mind likes to be kept on its' toes. Think of your mind like a girlfriend/boyfriend, you can't go too long without a few surprises or new experiences.

Meditate. I can't stress this enough. It can really take you out of your element and enlighten you to new solutions to past problems (creative and otherwise). The place your mind goes during meditation is the place where creative ideas come from. Give it a try. The first couple of weeks you might just have a bunch of thoughts bouncing around trying to organize themselves, but soon enough those thoughts will start to quiet and you'll then experience something completely new.

If you are stuck on a music idea, I suggest you hunt down Brian Eno's *Oblique Strategies* cards.

For iPhone users there is a free application as well. Just search the app store. This is a good description of what these cards do...

"Oblique Strategies cards came about when Brian Eno and Peter Schmidt discovered that they both kept a set of basic working principles to guide them through moments of pressure during the creative process. They became aware that the pressures involved in producing creative work on a schedule caused them to no longer stick to productive modes of thinking/creating. These strategies are one way they devised to help them get around the problem of becoming stuck in the creative process -- when stuck, consult the cards, and then continue with the creative process after considering the card."

I've got no problem with drug or drink enhanced creativity, but just remember that it's opening a door that you can tap into sober, and without the side effects. I personally have given up drugs and don't even drink caffeine. I drink alcohol on occasion, but not too much. I think I am coming up with much better ideas *now* than I did in the past. I certainly don't regret my past, but I prefer to create from a state of sobriety. There isn't a wrong or right choice, just be sure you are both being productive without being self destructive.

When to give up on music

Ever have those feelings that you're getting nowhere with your songs. Perhaps you listen to a song on the radio or in a club and just think "there is no way I'm going to be this good". Maybe you're having a hell of a time learning a new piece of equipment or software. Maybe the technical side of things has you overwhelmed your ideas just seem uninspired. Maybe you are feeling like whatever gift you had for this, you've lost. Maybe you've never felt you've had a gift for making music.

It would be fair to say that once you've had a few accomplishments under your belt, your confidence improves. It's definitely a good feeling to do something that gets attention and a pat on the back (even if it's from your own hand). Unfortunately, after the buzz from that accomplishment has come and gone, you start to question whether or not you can do it again.

Maybe your early musical accomplishments were a fluke. You start to wish you could bottle up that formula and pour a little on everything you did, but of course if that worked everybody would be cranking out smash after smash.

Some people become afraid to branch out and explore new musical territory. They've got a reputation to uphold and they just can't fail. This can create long periods of writers' block (which is really just the fear of sucking turned into a lack of inspiration).

The fact of the matter is that whether you are a beginner or a veteran, you are going to have creative spurts followed by lulls. It's natural and is nothing to be afraid of. It's the natural flow of things.

For me, I'll just be messing around with a groove and things will start to get interesting. Pretty soon I'll have added enough parts to make a pretty sweet 32 bar loop. I'll play this in my headphones over and over getting really pumped about what I've made and then I'll let it be for the night. I'll go to sleep feeling confident and totally in flow with my creativity. A day or two might pass before I open up the song again, and all of a sudden things just don't sound as cool as

I remember. It sounds like somebody came in and messed it up. Next comes the complete confidence crash. All those fears of not being good enough come out. This feeling sucks.

It's pretty natural to be uninspired when this is the vibe we are bringing to the table day in and day out. There are several things you can do outside of throwing in the towel though and I'd like to discuss some of them. Some approaches may directly conflict with another approach, so feel free to pursue the one that vibes with you most.

Keep Going

Being stuck in the unfinished song syndrome is the point that separates the boys from the men (or girls from the women). With any worthy pursuit you are going to hit a few walls. This is just a way that life filters out those who aren't worthy of the prize. If you've been a quitter in the past, all that is required of you is to stand back up and have another go.

Keep this in mind...

If you haven't had these feelings of being a failure, you probably haven't accomplished much.

Roadblocks are actually a way of knowing that you are reaching beyond your comfort zone. I actually look at it as a good thing, an old friend. Welcome it willingly and you can transform it into an ally. It's those things that feel uncomfortable at first that can be the birth of some of your best work.

Yes, I understand that sometimes you will be in the full creative flow and bang out something great without much struggle and this is something we can always hope for, but to expect this type of flow as the norm is to miss the bigger picture of what an artist is and what an artist does. You have to embrace the bliss *and* the dirt, the feeling of being lost and the joy of finding yourself again.

In nearly everything you do that is worthy of your time, you are going to lose the plot for a bit. You just want to make sure you allow yourself a breather to recharge if you are running on empty (more on this later).

Curiosity

Chances are you are taking this music thing way too seriously and it's taking the fun out of creating. One way that I like to recharge my batteries is to pursue curious experiments. For me this usually starts with a "I wonder what would happen if..." One experiment was to see how many ways I could process one loop through different effect chains to create an evolving part that kept me interested for, say, fifteen minutes. This might not turn into a song in the end, but it very well might be a joyful pursuit that might put a few more tools in you creative toolbox. It might inspire you or boost your confidence, and at the very best might turn into a great piece of music.

The great thing about curiosity is that it doesn't take itself too seriously and it doesn't expect or require perfection. Instead it puts you "in the moment" and just allows whatever happens to happen. Brian Eno (I know, him again. What can I say? He's brilliant!) is known to spend most of his time setting up an experimental process for music to just happen on its own. I like this approach, especially when I am feeling uninspired. I just create a process that allows the music to make itself, until I decide to take a more active role in it again (if that even becomes necessary). Sometimes if you stop trying to control music, it starts to evolve almost on its own. You almost become more of a witness to what is taking place.

Think of creative ideas as something that is "out there" in the cosmos. Every idea that can be thought and every song that can be made is already there. You are not the maker of music. You are simply a vessel in which music comes through.

Mozart had a very similar experience of music. He felt that he was simply given full works of music, already completed. His job was simply to get out of the way and write down what had come to him.

When we realize that we are not the makers of music, we can put more of our focus on getting ourselves in tune with the source of the ideas. Obviously, expressing these ideas efficiently will require some skills and proper tools, but you can always find someone who has the skills you currently lack.

Take a break

The real question is whether you are putting yourself in a state of mind that makes you feel inspired or if you're giving in to mundane daily habits that are uninspiring. When many of us feel uninspired, we find ourselves constantly thinking about our lack of drive and feeling guilty about pursuing our many distractions. We often try to keep close to home "just in case" inspiration strikes, thus continuing the path of an uninspired life.

A better approach is to allow yourself to quit making music for a bit. Take away the option of making music and give yourself a month or even longer to pursue other interests, guilt free. Maybe you want to travel, write a book, learn to become a better cook, expand your social network (preferably face to face), or learn a new language.

When you stop feeling guilt for not being musically creative, you can pursue many other aspects of your life with much less resistance. Everybody needs a break to recharge their batteries, and many of us never do that. We become convinced that somehow running on dead batteries will eventually lead us to our best work. In reality, if we look at most, if not all, of our favorite artists, we find they draw inspiration from a variety of life experiences. Allow yourself to quit making music for a bit and fill your empty cup by getting out and doing life. It's a good idea to keep a notebook and/or a recorder close at hand. When the ideas come back to you, they tend to come on strong.

Work with a partner

I find that working with another person can really help bring out the best in each other. It's good to work with someone who has strengths that are your weaknesses and vice versa. I've found that I might hit a creative high when my partner is at a low, or they can pick up the slack when I've hit a breaking point. If you don't currently have a person to work with, consider finding someone, preferably in your local area. If that is a no go, you can always find someone online that you can send files back and forth to. Although it won't be quite the same as working with someone in the same room, technology has made this pretty seamless.

When all else fails, allow yourself to suck

That's right, if you can't seem to get anything good out of yourself, enjoy the process of sucking. See how bad you can make something. Do all the wrong things and enjoy it. Laugh with your inner critic because you can both agree "Yes, this is *really* embarrassing". Keep going, make it worse! Embrace the suck in you. It's liberating!

Eventually, you will find yourself enjoying the process and having a laugh. You may even find that you hit a roadblock in your suckiness, and simply can't come up with a way to suck any worse. You might even accidentally do something that sounds good. As you go through this process, you will find that you are in one of the best mental states for being creative, and as you are riding that wave you may even have the drive to open up one of those unfinished songs and push it a little further.

Get Creative

Creativity and your left and right brain functions

Let's talk about how to be more productive by not only using your right and left brain functions correctly, but also using them in the right sequence. You might not be aware that how you separate your functions in any creative endeavor can make all the difference in how easy and enjoyable the creative experience is. The more enjoyable and relaxing the experience is, the more your mind will gravitate toward being inspired, thus more creative output as well as a more authentic personal expression.

Let's take a look at some words to best describe the left and right side of the brain:

Left brain:

- Logical

- Detail oriented

- Fact oriented

- Interprets words and language

- Mathematical and scientific

- Order and pattern perception

- Strategic

- Practical

The left brain functions are often more associated with right handed people. The left brain is great with details, organizing and quality control. You would want to use the left brain when planning out ideas, figuring out which tools are going to be best for the job, and guesstimating how much time something might take. In musical terms, these are some things you may want to put your left brain to work doing:

- Creating templates that will best work for the type of music you create. This would include FX you would most likely use and sounds you may need access to. Having this done keeps you from having to slow down or stop altogether when you are in a creative groove.

- Making sure all of your studio wiring and routing is complete. This will give you easy access to your hardware and software.

- Getting all of your samples and loops at easy access

- Checking all of your recording levels

- Creating a music friendly mood with proper lighting and aroma. Also making sure you don't have any distracting noises that can interfere with your concentration or recording process.

Right Brain:

- Feeling oriented

- "Big picture" oriented

- Interprets sounds, symbols and images

- Philosophical and spiritual

- "Out of the box" thinking

- Inspiration oriented

- Imaginative

- Risk taking

- Deals with the realm of possibility

The right brain is vital to the creative process, and if it is allowed to create uninterrupted and without left brained second guessing, you can expect a fantastic creative experience. The right brain needs to flow freely with ideas without judgement. Creating for ten minutes and then analyzing for the next twenty minutes is like driving in stop and go traffic. It is counterproductive and frustrating.

The right brain is best at these functions:

- Messing with loops, samples and sounds uninterrupted

- Getting "lost" in the music

- Experimenting

- Mixing and panning

- Real time or "in the moment" creativity

Given how each side of the brain functions so differently, it is very important to put each side to work in the proper order so that one side doesn't interfere with the other.

Let's take a look at one way to approach creating music while keeping the information above in mind.

Start with the right brain:

This is where you dream up an idea. You don't have to have a song idea in mind at all. The point of this process is to prime your mind for creativity by giving it a clear direction.

Spend a few minutes imagining your desired audience listening to and enjoying your new song. Imagine, or even physically create the way your CD cover might look. Perhaps you can imagine your song getting rave reviews in magazines.

The point is to get yourself in the mental state of mind that you are not only capable but also quite talented and creative at what you do. You don't want to get into the creative process thinking "Well crap, I hope I can at least finish *something*". It's much better to get yourself to the phase of "This song is gonna knock 'em dead!"

If you think of all the people who seem to crank out hit after hit (not that I'm saying a hit song should be your aim) it's got to strike you that these guys are able to keep that creative excitement because they have experienced the positive results of their work in the past. You are going to have to create this in your head. This may sound like a silly step, but give it a shot, you might be surprised.

Get yourself organized:

This is the part that your left brain loves, so let it play.

In this step you will get organized by creating song templates. In these templates you will want to create plenty of audio and midi tracks loaded with instruments and sounds you are most likely to use. You will also want to set up some send FX with a couple of good reverbs, delay and compression (or whatever is important for you creating your type of music).

Check all of your cables from any hardware, sound cards, external hard drives, midi controllers, and monitors. Make sure you have any microphones set up and ready to go when needed, and amp settings dialed in etc.

Make sure your recording levels are good, and your recording environment is set up for inspiration and creative flow. Make sure you have access to any samples, loops or other resources as well.

Make sure your workspace is clean. A mess rarely inspires.

The whole point of this is so once you start creating, you will have no obstacles slowing you down or stopping your process.

Have you ever been so involved in reading a book that you no longer realize you are reading words, that you are instead seeing imagery? Have you ever been interrupted and find it hard to get back to the "zone" you were just in? This is what we want to do our best to avoid when you are in that musical zone. It can be tough to get yourself there to begin with, and even tougher once you have a roadblock or technical issue slowing you down.

Time to Create.

This is where all this work is going to really pay off by letting your right brain do what it was meant to do. Just play and experiment. Throw things around, mess with sounds, have fun with samples, loops and rhythms. Don't worry about trying to be a genius, just realize that the genius will come out when you just let yourself have some fun without any second guessing.

It's best to just record everything you do, because often it's the mistakes that end up being your best most unique sounds and give your music some real personality. Don't even worry too much about creating a song, simply enjoy making sounds and taking note of what strikes your interest. Continue to do this for as long as you enjoy it. By the end of this, you should have a few inspiring parts to work with.

Copy, Paste, Delete.

You have let your creative mind play, and have come up with a few ideas that you like. This is about the time you are going to want to let your left brain back in make some judgement calls.

The important thing is that you don't get too attached to any of your noodling around. Just accept that some things are gonna stay and some things need to go. Don't take too much time with this, the less second guessing the better. Your mind processes things much faster than you are consciously aware, so just go with your gut feeling. Listen to something and decide quickly, stay or go.

You will quickly find your most inspiring work and get rid of anything that would end up cluttering your music. Just roll with it and enjoy the process. Don't let yourself get caught up on one or two sounds or loops. You need to manage your ideas first, then you get to create again once you have your best pieces.

Arrange.

Arranging your ideas and adding parts as necessary is going to be a balance between left and right brain functions. Don't get yourself too lost in your head, but also don't do too much second guessing (as you can see, I think second guessing is usually a bad thing and counter productive).

If you are finding yourself stuck, feel free to listen to another song and borrow some of the arrangement ideas. You aren't attempting to make everything perfect, but more trying to create the big picture.

At the end of this process, you should know how long your song is going to be and have your overall arrangement in order. You should also see where the gaps are in your song that will need to be filled.

Fill the gaps.

Here you will add the parts that are missing to your arrangement by getting right brain creative but left brain practical. You'll want to get your reverb and delays dialed in as well as compression and creative effects.

You will also want to get your parts EQ'd and strip away unwanted frequencies in each sound to remove mud and keep everything clean. You want to get yourself prepared and organized for the mixing phase.

Mixing.

Mixing should be a very right brained function and should be perhaps one of the most enjoyable parts of the creative process.

You'll want to relax yourself into the vibe of the song and get the levels and panning placed. Don't be tempted to simply pan things where you usually do (although there are some rules you may want to keep in mind). It's better to play with a few channels that work well together and set your levels and pan until you feel some kind of shift in yourself.

You should start to feel like you are getting a bit lost in the music. This is a very good sign. It's usually best to start with your drums and bass and work up from that format. Then you may want to also try mixing from the most inspiring sounds down to the background sounds. You may find some interesting results.

How to Work with Creative Ease

Many of us get stuck at some point in the song writing process before getting anything across the finish line, and I've found one of the major triggers in getting blocked.

I discovered this secret in an odd way, so to explain it to you, I'll have to share a bit more about myself. It's something I've been dealing with for quite a while, and it's been both frightening and at times embarrassing.

I used to suffer from a pretty severe panic disorder that has manifested into too many awful symptoms to discuss here without getting completely off topic. (Stay with me though, there is a point to all this).

In 2010, quite out of the blue, I developed a crippling fear of driving on freeways. I knew it made no sense to suddenly feel this intense fear, but a switch went off in my brain like a splinter in the mind. I would literally have nightmares of waking up in my car, driving 70 mph down the freeway having no idea how I got there. Of course I would jolt awake in a cold sweat.

Not long after, I had to drive from Denver to Iowa City, where I was living at the time. I agonized about each lane switch, on ramp, off ramp, overpass, and those moments of feeling pure claustrophobia.

Not long after this, something clicked for me. Something that I'd be able to use in other aspects of my life, and now I'll share that with you.

The things that are easy in your life are processed as one simple task, while the things you dread fill your head with all kinds of seemingly complicated details.

Let me give you an example:

Let's say a friend asked me to meet her for lunch fifteen minutes out of town. To my friend, there is no second thought. He simply thinks "Right, I'll drive over to this cool new sushi place".

On the other hand, this is what is going on in my head:

- "Oh great, that means I have to get on the freeway. Is a semi-truck going to run me off the road when I try to get on?"

- "How many lane changes will I have to make?"

- "How many freeway changes will require me to be in the fast lane?"

- "Are there any scary overpasses?"

- "Will I have a freak out and have to turn around and go home, leaving my friend high and dry?"

- "What is the parking going to be like? Will I get lost searching for parking?"

And on and on.

As you can see, the way my mind processes a simple drive for lunch is *far* different than the average person. Thankfully I am beginning to overcome this fear by leaps and bounds.

So, how does this apply to music?

When you get stuck on your music, you aren't thinking of things as one little chunk (create a breakdown). Instead, you are projecting a disaster into your future (like I did with the driving). You may be thinking:

- "This part of the song is too complicated to accomplish."

- "How long does this break have to be?"

- "What sounds do I use and which do I remove for a proper breakdown?"

- "Crap, now I have to create chord changes on every track for this break. That's just overwhelming."

- "I have to design a new sound to add an additional dynamic. Designing the perfect sound is really hard."

- "How do I create a massive swoosh at the end?"

By this time, you have psyched yourself out before you even started. You brain is expecting failure, or at the very least a confusing and unpleasant experience.

Can you see why you would get blocked?

On the other hand, maybe you are great at getting an 8 bar groove going. Even though there are a lot of details involved in creating a drum riff, bassline and a hook of some sort, you simply think of it in your mind as "creating a groove". No fear there, you're just messing around.

When writing, I go through both phases. The flow and the blocks. Today I am in the flow. In my head and on my "To Do" list, it is simply "Write the book". The details aren't even really considered. I had the subject in mind and just knew that I had enough to say to get through it without getting stuck.

I am learning to internalize this vibe so I can reboot it in the future.

How can you clear your creative blocks?

- Identify what thoughts are running through your head. How many steps do you perceive it'll take to get from A to Z?

- Write down the way your mind processes the tasks that need to be completed.

- Highlight all the steps and negative thoughts that create stress for you.

- Write down ten ways you can make each step easier for yourself. Some answers may sound ridiculous. Write them down anyway. Don't look outside yourself. You are a problem solving machine when you allow yourself to be.

- Return to your list daily adding to the list until you find some solutions.

- When you find some solutions that work for you, start putting them into action until the habit is no longer stressful. This may take some time, but the more you work through it, the easier it gets.

These steps might seem way too basic, but you'll be surprised what you can do when you put your brain to work. Also, create a habit of recreating your successes in your head. Visualize the songs you finished, and begin to think of those successes as one process instead of all the little details. When in songwriting mode, try to stay in the moment. What you are actually doing in the moment is nearly always less stressful than what you are telling yourself it's going to be like.

Templates and tools

It helps tremendously to save any tools you create that simplifies the song writing process for you. No need to reinvent the wheel. When you think of writing a song you might break it down something like this.

- Create a looped groove that sounds exciting and fresh to me
- Create an intro
- Introduce chord structure and bass
- 1st break down
- Introduce a new melody or counter melody
- 2nd break down
- Peak energy of song
- Small break
- Stripped down groove
- Outro

Any tools and templates to help through this process will not only be a great timesaver, but will also turn something that was once stressful to something you find fun. This is the reason I created my Master Template for my digital audio workstation of choice (Ableton Live). It has turned the most stressful aspect of song writing in to a lot of fun, and has greatly improved my output as well as my customers.

"Write a new tune."

Doesn't that sound more calming then the chaotic thoughts you allow to run through your head? Keep coming to that, and when you get stuck don't try to figure out how others did it, try to see if you can come up with your own way. This will give you the benefit of developing your own sound instead of copying someone else. It's also a huge step toward building your song writing confidence.

Don't get me wrong, there is a time and place for learning from others, but don't turn it into a crutch and allow yourself to stop thinking.

You have creative genius in you and the world needs you to harness it.

Creative procrastination

When it comes to productivity, there is nothing the mind loves more than putting things off. Especially if it's creatively important. Because of this you may need to trick your mind into getting started.

There are a few ways to go about this, and I've mentioned a couple of approaches in past chapters. For a quick recap though, here are a couple ways to get yourself started.

- Just start - Don't prepare to start. Just jump in and don't ask permission or look for advice. Just act like you've already got things under control. You'll be surprised how powerful this can be on your creativity and productivity.

- 15 minutes a day - it's exactly as it sounds. It's a commitment over a certain period of time, typically thirty days, where you commit to doing a task for fifteen minutes a day without missing a day. You can go more than fifteen minutes each day, but that doesn't get you off the hook for tomorrow's fifteen minute commitment.

- An alternate approach is one I just read from one of my favorite bloggers, Steve Pavlina. He suggests you commit to doing a larger project in fifteen minute chunks. You simply commit to get busy for fifteen undistracted minutes. If after fifteen minutes you want to stop you are free to, or you can immediately re-commit to another fifteen minutes or after a short break. I think this is a fantastic approach.

- Keep a record - Another approach is to keep a log of everything you do for a full day. Anytime you change a task you write it down. So if you are working and then you get a text and you respond, write it down and write the time of day next to it. If you use the bathroom, write it down. Essentially what this does is makes you much more focused, and aware of how you are spending your time from moment to moment, and you can later determine where all your time is going. This tip is huge!

A new Approach

Here is another approach I've just come up with that should work wonders for you. One of my biggest roadblocks is the preparation before actually getting started with a task. For example, when making music you need to make sure you have all the correct equipment, sound card, midi controller etc. set up, as well as access to your sound library, pre-sets and templates. All of that can be very un-motivating when all you want to do is create. Typically you've lost your momentum half way into setting up. Unless your setup is dead simple, you typically will avoid setting up to create, and thus you avoid creating because you have to set up. It's a lose-lose situation.

Here is a very simple solution:

Devote fifteen minute chunks of time just setting up for making music. If fifteen minutes is all you can handle, cool, but you'll probably find that after the first fifteen minutes you'll have less resistance to the next fifteen minutes. When you are finally set up, *don't attempt to start creating.* Take the rest of the day off and then commit to fifteen minute chunks of musical work first thing the next morning if at all possible.

This takes away all the distractions and procrastination tactics you typically encounter, and gives you a direct path to starting work immediately. Also, do your best to shut off any programs or social media that will distract you, and clear your workspace from anything distracting as well.

The only thing that should be grabbing your attention is your project. Also if the setup is complex, you may want to take some notes to make it easier the next time you need to set up for a project.

If you have to tear down after a project, allow yourself to hold off until the next day. You may find you have some last minute ideas spark up, and you will want your workstation ready to go.

By separating the tasks of preparing to create and creating, you are giving yourself a huge advantage. First off, it's much easier preparing to create without fear of failure. You are not going to be judged for how you set up your equipment, so you'll have much less resistance getting yourself started.

The next day when you actually *do* create, the mundane tasks will already be completed, leaving you a direct path to take what is in your head and turn it into something physical without distractions or roadblocks. Separating the tasks takes away your ability to use either one as an excuse for not completing the other.

Give it a try if you find it hard to get started on a creative project. Some of these tips helped this book get written. I hope it helps you as well!

Exploring Happy Accidents

Ever notice how some of your favorite parts of your songs are the parts you didn't intentionally do in the first place? Ever record something "on the fly", and then attempt to recreate it "more professionally"?

From my experience, it's usually the unplanned part that I like more.

Have you ever been doodling around on a synth with whatever sound is on at the time expecting to change the sound later, but notice that you simply can't improve it because it sounds great as it is?

I have a theory on all this, and this of course is just my personal opinion and speculation, but I figured I would share it with you to see if you find it thought provoking.

I feel that the reason these "accidents" sound good to us is because it didn't sound like anything we would normally do. In fact often times it almost seems like it was played by somebody else altogether.

The fact of the matter is that we usually over analyze anything that we intentionally do, for example, most of us don't like the raw sound of our own voice, until we throw on a bunch of production techniques and effects until it sounds 'not' like us.

Another aspect of the "happy accident" is that in some ways, I don't think it's an accident at all. I think when we let go and get into our zone, we create from a higher level. It seems 'not' like us because we rarely experience this aspect of ourselves in daily life. I find that when I'm in that creative mode, that interesting synchronicities and accidents happen just when I was needing something to. This also makes the creative flow much more smooth and pleasant. I certainly wouldn't by any means call this masterful words of wisdom, but rather something to ponder...

Sometimes failures and accidents pave the road to your best work!

Is sampling a cop out for less creative people?

There has long been a debate in every form of art between making something from scratch vs sampling the work of others to create something new. One side would argue that all their ideas came from within, while the other is just copying what has already been done.

Who made what?

What is truly yours and what is truly mine when it comes to creating? To answer this, you would have to look to the source of ideas.

Where do ideas come from?

Many would say that great ideas don't have ownership, but rather pass through you from another place. Others would simply say that if it was in your head, then it's completely you. If you want to come from that angle, then where did "you" come from? Where did the "you" that is creating these wonderful things come from? Did you invent yourself?

Whatever we are has a source beyond ourselves in a physical space that we share. Humans invented ownership, but in reality, it doesn't exist. We are always sharing everything (energy, atoms, air, and sunshine).

All we are is filters. Each of us has a unique filter that takes in information in a unique way and puts something new back into the world. Some work really hard to develop this filter, and I think that deserves respect, but to say that something is purely your own is fairly delusional.

I read a lot of books that all tend to say the same thing, but because of the filter they come through and the effort to keep that filter pure, some books connect on a much deeper level than others. The content is not really unique, it's the filter that is *you* that makes it individualistic.

When I was younger, I woke up to music when MTV was introduced (yeah, that channel that is known only for reality TV now. Yeah them. They used to be 24/7 music videos, and it was *amazing*). I saw Billy Idol, Duran Duran, Echo and the Bunnymen, U2 and Devo among many others and thought "I want to do *that!*"

In my opinion, from that point on, there would be nothing truly original that would come out of me. Instead it would be a mishmash of all those things I like about music. Unconsciously I would be sampling a drum rhythm from here, a bass idea from there and a guitar riff from somewhere else. Of course the tone of each would also be influenced by my tastes. Sure, I might stumble upon some happy accidents that help shape my sound, but the source would always be outside of myself.

Maybe you had a music teacher, or a friend you would trade ideas with. Sure you might go your own way, but the influence will always be there, even if it's "God, I hope I never sound like that. He's cool and all, but I would never play music like *that*".

At what level is sampling considered taboo?

- Is it ok to play a riff influenced from another source, as long as you aren't directly sampling from the original artist?

- Is it ok to sample a drum hit or a horn sound, but not a loop?

- Is it ok to grab a loop, as long as it's obscure?

- Is it ok to sample whole songs, like a DJ does, as long as he is creating something new with his mixes?

- It is ok to play someone else's mashup in a set?

- Is it ok to play a song that has scratching in it, or must you be the only one performing scratches?

- Is it ok to sample your own work and then mime to it, if the show is too important to risk messing up?

Sampling as an art in and of itself

Like him or hate him, Andy Warhol was a very popular artist who built a career sampling what was around him and repurposing it. Were the pieces used *already* art, or did he inject something into it that made you look at the work and go "Ah yes, that's definitely a Warhol piece".

Some great albums were made from samples and hold up as great works themselves. Several bands come to mind.

- *Beck*
- *Beastie Boys* (particularly Licensed to Ill and Paul's Boutique)
- *Pop Will Eat Itself*
- *Thievery Corporation*
- *Daft Punk*
- *Fatboy Slim*
- *The KLF*
- *Chemical Brothers*
- *Prodigy*
- *Pogo*
- *Oasis* (ok, they didn't directly sample, but they certainly borrowed ideas heavily)

I'm sure many of you can name loads more. In my opinion, when an artist creates something that is greater than the sum of the pieces used to make it, it has merit as art and deserves its' place. If a song is a hit only because of some Hall and Oates sample it used and is otherwise forgettable, I'd consider that a bit of a cop out.

You know something is good when you are no longer concerned about how something was made or what specific tools were used, but because you're lost in the sound.

Want to reinvent the wheel?

I would say that sampling is using something someone else made to make a work of your own. This would mean that if you didn't invent everything you are using, you're more or less sampling. The guitar or piano you're playing. The plugin you're using. The computer and DAW you're using. Hell you might as well make your own electricity while you're at it.

Music is a bit like evolution, it borrows from the past while testing out new possibilities. The strong ones may split off to a new species, or for music, a new genre.

What are you really afraid of?

I think people who are opposed to sampling have this paranoia that someone is going to get a result more easily than the last generation did, by "borrowing" and repurposing old ideas. They might be afraid this it will make all their hard work obsolete with some simple copy and paste action.

Everything becomes a little easier for the next generation. Think about how information is gathered via the internet. What a fantastic resource! More or less resources aren't a factor in determining who is an artist or not. The great ones will always shine through regardless.

I'd say that this is really great motivation to remain relevant in what you do and to keep pushing yourself forward. If you are really good at what you do, you will always be ahead of people who are sampling from you. Then again, you might find that those who sample from you add a spin that in turn re-inspires your new work.

Creativity never stops unless you just aren't cut out for this profession. Don't be upset that music is being borrowed, sampled, stolen and re-purposed; be happy that the evolution of sound never ends.

Talent and Theory

Make music now. Talent not required

- To those of you who listen to music but are afraid to attempt to grasp the music making process.

- To all the people who may have toyed with the idea of creating music but quickly realized that their natural abilities are far too limited.

- To all the people who have dreamed of stepping on a stage in a packed room but lack the ability to lead a room of spectators on a worthwhile journey.

- To all of you who have picked up an instrument, plucked, pressed or blew a hideous noise, set the instrument down and slowly backed away.

- To those who think they'll never understand what all those crazy knobs on that synthesizer do.

- To all those who downloaded the trial version of a new software, gave their best attempt at something musical over the weekend, and then deleted the software by Monday in frustration.

- To all the people who didn't ask that technical question because "If I haven't figured this out yet, it's just not meant to be, so there is no point embarrassing myself".

- To all those who can't tell a wind instrument from a plucked instrument, between live drums and a drum machine, between echo and reverb or a quarter note from a triplet.

- To those who don't yet understand how a compressor helps some sounds gel together.

- To those who have heard of midi but have no idea what its purpose is.

- To all of those don't know the difference between an A Minor and C Major scale.

- To those who don't know what a pentatonic scale is.

- To those who don't even know what a scale is.

- To those not familiar with middle C and where to find it on a piano.

- To those who think or have been told they can't make music until they have mastered music theory.

- To those who can't tell if there's a little too much upper midrange on that mix down, or too much mud around 500 Hz.

I want to tell you with as much sincerity as I can muster that I was once where you are. My musical vocabulary was nil. I couldn't distinguish between a rock band and an all synth band as far as instrumentation. I couldn't read or write music notation (and still can't). I had poor rhythm and a hard time keeping my playing in tempo. I still only know a handful of chords, the rest I just make up by ear. To this day, the songs I write on guitar consist mostly of simple chords, or slight variations that sound good to me. I'm no virtuoso, but I don't find myself limited by my lack of chord book knowledge.

If you think that I must then have been a computer whiz, easily programming my ideas into something listenable, think again. I didn't even know how to properly turn off a computer, had no idea what a desktop or a folder was, and the concept of cut copy and paste was completely foreign to me. I'm still haunted by this calm confident sounding voice sample that came with my Sony (then Sonic Foundry) Sound Forge (Sound editing software) that said "Sound editing keeps getting easier and easier". Every time I heard that guy's voice, I wanted to throw my computer out of a window.

Still to this day, I when I start a new song, I have a childlike naivety and curiosity in the process. I don't know my scales, and I still create my music by ear. My writing process consists of a few approaches.

- Listen to what I've already got and wait for a musical idea to come to my head then sound it out by ear.

- Duplicate a melodic midi file, change the sound, raise or lower by an octave, move notes around until it sounds good.

- Dick around until I've stumbled across something that sounds interesting

Obviously, the more you write, the better your instincts and musical vocabulary become. You become better able to tell if something doesn't sound quite right or if you've nailed it. There is usually a point at which I accept not being perfect and let it be. Like Da Vinci said "Art is never finished, only abandoned". This idea of perfection is not only elusive to the amateurs, but also the masters.

I'm not trying to embarrass myself here, although I simply don't care how others view my knowledge or lack thereof. I want you to think of this complete lack of knowledge as your first stepping stone to mastery. It honestly doesn't matter where you start, only where you want to get to. Tell me one thing you're doing now that you didn't at one point know absolutely nothing about.

I'll wait...

Don't ever think you can only create music when you stop having questions. Questions create possibilities where there once weren't any. The day people stop asking questions is the day music runs out of ideas. I believe that having good taste in music is much more of a priority than having skill. If you have taste in music, you will recognize when you aren't quite where you want to be yet, and that will drive you to improve. As you improve, your listening will also improve, and you'll find yourself noticing details in music that previously eluded you, thus driving you forward once again. It becomes an upward spiral.

There is only one qualification for making music. Because you want to.

Why I don't Learn Music Theory

Music to me is mysterious and magical. Without restriction, I can explore music through trial and error and come to my own conclusions, as well as make my own discoveries. I enjoy playing guitar or my keyboard and fingering out variations of simple chords until I hear something that excites me. It gives me this wonderful boost of energy. It's that "Wow cool, I just discovered something new!" feeling. I still get that to this day.

I can still recall regularly walking over a mile to the music store as a kid just to play the sounds on the amazing Roland Juno 60 synth. I had no idea how this instrument was creating such wonderful sounds. All I knew is that when a played a couple of keys, it sounded fantastic. As the years went by I eventually bought the Roland Juno 106 which was largely the same sound engine. Little by little I discovered what certain knobs did to the sound. I certainly didn't know what *all* of the knobs did. I just knew that when I pushed up that fader, it sounded even better.

As time went on, by default, I gained a bit more musical experience and started understanding what was previously behind the curtain. Soon enough I started to lose a bit of the magic because I knew the tricks. When you know the magician's (or musician's) tricks, they no longer drive the imagination the same way.

I had to set the synth down for a while and rediscover the magic in the guitar. While working with the synth, I was able to forget and unlearn some of what I know about the guitar. I felt like a beginner again. It felt new again. Like I was starting over for the first time. That was extremely exciting for me. I've always liked the "Give me four chords and an imagination" approach. I like to drop an instrument when I feel too comfortable on it for a while and explore something new.

When I was first given one of my dad's guitars, he also gave me a chord book. I tried, honestly I did. All I got was bored... and sore fingers. None of the music I was listening to were using these chords anyway. I then thought of all the guitar players at my school

103

who played much better than me, and realized that although I was impressed by their playing, I wasn't impressed with what sounded to me like a cookie cutter approach to writing songs. I imagined them arguing "No, it's gotta be *this* chord, anyone who knows music knows *that*!" Sometimes getting it all wrong can have pleasant results.

Listening to *Bauhaus*, *The Cure* and *New Order* were much more exciting to me even though there were no elaborate guitar solos. I knew these bands didn't play their instruments as well, but there was something else they did have that sparked my imagination much more.

My argument is not that one style of music is better than another. It's that sometimes when you create your own path, it may take longer, but it's more likely that you'll find your own sound, and in doing so, a much deeper satisfaction.

Would you prefer to know all the chords in existence, and lose that feeling of discovering them on your own? Would you prefer to play that one chord because your education has taught you that it's appropriate, or because it feels good to you? Education can be pretty important to understand some of the rules before you break them, but letting go and using "the force" might help you express things that simply can't be taught.

For me, every time I sit down to make music, I still get to feel like a beginner in this magical and mysterious world. Of course I get better instincts which help me solve problems faster, but it's very satisfying to know that I made these discoveries on my own or through conversations with others of similar tastes. There is still a bit of fear that I might suck or that I might not know how something I want to accomplish is done, but the problem solving involved in making music is one of the things that drives me creatively. After all these years, I wouldn't trade what I don't know about music for anything. My ignorance has been bliss. Bring on the magicians!

Here's a few musicians who never learned music theory:

- *David Bowie* (except for sax lessons)
- *The Beatles*
- *Eric Clapton* (he started learning only recently)
- *Brian Eno*
- *Thelonious Monk*
- *William Orbit*
- *David Byrne*
- *Aphex Twin*
- *Danny Elfman*

Is technical talent truly inspiring?

I recall watching a live performance of "Shadowplay" by *Joy Division* from 1978 on YouTube. The performance was raw, the playing was amateur and the vocals were out of key and...

It was *still* amazing.

I proceeded to read the comments below and was pleasantly surprised that 90% of the comments were also praising the performance. Only one person mentioned the lack of technical skill and everybody jumped down his throat.

Then of course everyone was dogging the cover version of this song by *The Killers* basically calling them a bunch of hacks. Now technically speaking, *The Killers* version could easily be considered better. It was sonically recorded and mixed better, the instruments were well played and the vocals were on key... but nobody cared. Now I'm not here to say *The Killers* are shit, but rather I want to explore why bands like *Joy Division, Bauhaus* and *The Cure* are practically worshipped despite their lack of what some would call musicianship.

Why are bands like these so well respected despite (or perhaps even because of) a lack of technical talent? What is that magic formula? Why is it that we excuse their lack of technical talent and in fact rate them much higher than bands that clearly have better musicianship?

Some of you reading this will simply say these bands are completely over-rated, or popular for being popular in the underground. I'm going to have to say that I believe there is more to it, and I would like to explore this a bit deeper.

Being a proud non-musician myself, I enjoy the idea of mucking about on an instrument like a curious child. If I already felt I knew everything there was to know, I probably wouldn't be very interested in making music. I suppose what I do mocks people that slave over their instrument of choice, but I don't think that is the whole picture. I, in fact, *have* slaved over music, but the things I am interested in are how to convey a vibe.

Sometimes pure talent shows little humanity.

Often, talent is something you hide behind. Nakedness and vulnerability can evoke much more emotion. I personally think it takes bravery to stand up on a stage with little but a handful of chords and some ideas that you want to get across.

Don't get me wrong, there are times when you need talent to convey a complex idea and those are amazing moments, but those moments are not driven by the desire to "show off" talent, but rather to get your message across as accurately as possible.

There is also something to be said about having pent up emotion and being a bit frustrated that you can't express it accurately. I think I can hear this in bands like *Nirvana* and *Joy Division*. Those bands were very vulnerable, and spoke for so many who were afraid to speak for themselves. Those who were afraid of their own normality. We can see ourselves in those who show themselves, warts and all.

It might be safe to say that those who are true fans of music don't base what is good on pure talent, but rather on how the music hits them whether it be *Mozart, The Who* or *Velvet Underground*. I think it's likely that "musicians" might get off on complexity for complexity's sake, because having the skill to learn it can be an ego boost in the same way as mastering a difficult video game. However, music is in a completely different field altogether. Some of the best music defies logic. Sometimes the words are nonsense and the simple parts that construct the song are laughable, yet we still find something intriguing about it.

I like to think that there is more that goes into music than just the instruments and vocals. I think there is something that gets recorded between the notes that weaves through the empty gaps. A sort of "ghost in the machine". I believe emotion and intention comes through the music, and those subtleties are picked up by those who really "listen" and "feel" the music.

Although all of my examples in this book are talking about live bands, I think the same "ghosts" can come through in electronic music as well. All instruments whether played by hand or programmed are soul-less until the soul is injected into it.

Musical Meditation

I have the ability to build a song idea in my head. Let's call it *"Musical Meditation"*.It can start from a riff, a drum pattern or a lyrical phrase. I can "hear" inside my head what works and what doesn't.

For example, I can try out certain vocal harmonies in my head, and hear how slight variations can create a better or worse result. I can tell if something will sound too full or too empty before I've physically played or sung a note. Sometimes I don't know exactly what is missing, but I know it's not quite "right".

Although I have this ability, I don't actually use it as often as I should.

The main reason is that I find it works better for me when I'm making guitar based songs. I figure electronic songs are more difficult because the soundscape is largely unfamiliar. I think many composers are so great at dreaming up symphonies because they are intimately familiar with each instrument that would make up a symphonic piece of music.

I was thinking about this today and pondering how I could develop this skill of mine, and perhaps help others develop it as well.

Here is an approach that I've come up with:

Dreaming up sounds

In order to accurately get a unique sound that is in your head into your computer or recording device, you are going to need to understand the fundamentals of sound.

- Try going into a synth and only use one oscillator.

- Turn off the filters and effects and just listen to each type of waveform: Sine, Square, Triangle, and Saw.

These are the basic sound palettes to every sound you will create. Understand these basics and you have the fundamentals to dreaming up great sounds, and being able to put the sound in your head into an actual song.

Although getting sidetracked can lead to some wonderfully surprising sounds, for this exercise it's of utmost importance that you see this process through without losing focus. I think it can be argued that this loss of focus is one of the leading causes of not completing songs.

Here's the scenario

You had an original idea in your head but lost focus early on, and just went with whatever interesting sound jumped out at you first. Soon you are listening to a loop or collection of sounds over and over without anywhere to go. You have essentially lost your steam.

Although magical things can happen on accident when you are attempting to create something else, it's also good to understand how to approximate an inspiring idea in your head.

What if you were able to quickly get the ideas out of your head accurately before you lost focus? My guess is that you would probably find more satisfaction in your work. Then of course once you got the basic idea out of your head you could allow for more experimentation and happy accidents.

Remember, this isn't a lesson in inflexibility, but of focus.

Having trouble dreaming up your own sounds? Try dreaming up someone else's.

- Pull up a song in your computer.

- Listen to just one tone that attracts you.

- When you find a sound you like, listen to it as closely as possible.

- Listen to how the sound characteristics change with each note.

- If there are volume variations, take note of those too.

Breaking it down.

If the sound you are trying to recreate in your head is complex, break it down into the separate parts that make the sound up.

If you have a hard time doing this, think of it as three different sounds. One sound in the lower frequency, one in the mid frequency and one in the high frequency. In the same way you might break down a harmony into each separate voice, many sound designers and musicians break down sounds to their most basic elements. When you can mentality break sounds down to their basic elements, you can better predict how to build your own complex tones as well.

Now that you have that sound in your head, close your eyes and try to vividly recreate that sound in your head. Try to hear it all by itself instead of in the context of a song. You may want to give this sound a name so you can mentally access it more easily.

Recreate the part you heard in your head in as much detail as possible.

Variation.

Next try changing some notes around and creating variations. Try not to lose the image in your head and don't change the sound in your head. It's very easy to get bored and wander off, but what we are trying to do is ingrain this sound into your memory as vividly as possible so you can add it to your mental palette.

Imagine changing the EQ, or filtering out the high frequencies, then the low frequencies.

Imagine the sound with a bit of distortion, flange, delay or reverb. If you can't vividly imagine these effects, you may want to spend some time adding these effects to some basic sounds so your mind has something to work with.

Practice makes perfect.

When you are able to do this with some proficiency, you will be able to add more and more instruments in your head and know how to get close to the sound you want before you've even played a note. You'll be able to build and arrange full song ideas in your head and work out the kinks before you waste any time in the studio.

In the same way that it takes a while to become good at meditating and blocking out all of the days thoughts, it's also difficult to start using "musical meditation" to focus on an idea without distractions. You may not get it right immediately, but with practice I am confident you will have an amazingly powerful tool that will just continue to get better and better.

The power of immediacy, and how to develop your sound

I am always thinking about the creative process. Especially when things aren't working. I still work on songs that kick my butt sometimes and I have had to ponder why that is. I'll be the first to admit that I've got strengths and weaknesses in my own creative process.

See, I come from a background of being a guitar player with a fascination for electronics. By the time I was in high school, I wanted to be a synth player, but my dad was a guitarist and gave me an electric guitar, so that's what I played...for a while.

The thing about guitar versus synths, is that there was an immediacy to it. I didn't have to dick around so much with the sound (in fact, most of the songs I played were variations of about 5 or 6 pre-sets I made). Once I had an idea, I was immediately able to play it with a satisfying sound. I realized that once I had a good tone, I could play endless ideas. This meant that I never really bothered with much sound design at all. I had my tone, and I knew it would always work within the sound of my band.

That began to change when I fell in love with fully electronic club music. So many sounds, so many choices. So much excitement. So much to learn.

So I was in a situation that I would guess many of you are in. In my case, I didn't realize there was a problem until I tried to write with the same immediacy as I did when I played guitar.

Guitar is like vanilla, not because it's bland, but it pretty much will go with anything and still sound reasonably good. Making electronic music was a different beast altogether.

Just because something sounded great on its own, didn't mean it would fit with other electronic sounds in a mix. In fact, picking the right sounds had become the greatest contributor to whether a song would sound amazing or like total crap. You can have amazing musical ideas, but if you put the wrong sounds together it'll sound amateur, and nobody will want to play your song.

You need the right sounds that work on a dance floor, and your production skills have got to be good.

Where people in bands learn their one instrument inside and out, many producers have to be a one man band excelling in all the instruments, while attempting to create a unique sound palette out of the literally millions of choices. It's ok to analyze the sound palette on a certain genre of music, but try not to copy one specific artist too strongly or you run a serious risk of sounding like a budget version of someone else's sound.

If there is one thing I have learned through my long music career, it's to choose the style you want to get exceptionally good at and don't lose focus. You can only get better at your thing when you stop trying to switch your style every time you hear a song you like. Of course you can be influenced and I would encourage that, but make sure you are developing your style & not wondering in too many directions (at least not until you've become proficient at your main style). I've been guilty of this as well, so I know how hard it can be to make a firm decision on what you want people to know you for.

You can always change your mind, or do side projects with other producers, but it make more sense to get really good at one thing instead of average (or below average) at several things.

If you are still struggling to find your sound, I suggest you start by build your palette.

What would your palette need? I can't speak for you, but I can make some suggestions:

- Drums/percussion
- Bass/Subs
- Pads/strings
- Stabs
- Leads

- Melodic sounds

- Effects

Try making 3-5 presets in each category and test them with each other. If something is not working nice with the other sounds, it either needs to be tweaked, or it needs to go. Soon enough, you will have all the sounds you need to make music, and will have dialed in the proper EQ's and effects that work with your style.

When you reach this point, you will have the immediacy you need for making music much more quickly, with the confidence that this sound palette will work for you time and time again. You can always expand your palette of course, but the more gradually this happens, the more proficient you will be with your tools.

So where are you at? Have you built yourself a workable template or are you drowning in an ocean of sound possibilities?

Simplify your choices to sounds that mix & match well with each other & you'll find it much easy to write songs that sound professional.

Finishing Music and Song writing

Producing is mostly problem solving

Many producers have a really difficult time looking at their own work and saying "This is done". There is a huge paranoia that there is a gaping hole in our work that is immediately going to be spotted by our peers. This issue can lead to analysis paralysis, and cause you to never finish anything you start.

Every track you show people will be a "work in progress". You'll never commit to saying "Here it is, it's done". I hope this information will help you across the finish line with more confidence.

The truth is, if you haven't written in a while, your songs may very likely have some unfinished business, but you really can't look at things like that. Your job is not to create perfection, it's to abandon your work when you've done all you can currently do.

See, your production improves in direct relationship with your experience and your listening skills. This means that unless you are willing to put yourself out there and possibly fail a few times, you will never truly begin to succeed. You'll think that one more learned trick is going to save your song, but it's really not the case.

You can't improve your skills from only studying somebody else's skills, unless you are also putting those skills to work. This is essential in developing your own style. You don't want to be chasing everybody else's.

When is my song done?

So when is your song complete then? The short answer is that it's done when you say it's done, but let me dive a bit deeper.

As you produce your own music, you start to develop a much better ear for things. You get much better at figuring out what makes other songs "tick", and learning to apply it to your own work. Many of us go through a period where we realize our song is still missing something. The problem is that we don't know *what*. Sometimes there truly is an element missing, other times the problem is in the mixing or EQ-ing. Other times there is just too much happening, and the song no longer sounds clean.

Once again, you learn this from *doing*. With any form of art, you can only be as good as you currently are.

So when is your song done? When you can no longer perceive any problems.

The problem solving approach

I have gained a decade of experience in a matter of months by writing constantly. I've written, remixed or collaborated on more than 60 songs so far, and still going strong. Surprisingly, I like most of my work. The advantage you have when you are continuously writing is that you are building habits, skills and instincts. You can also always go back to a previously "finished" song, and know immediately what you can do to make it better.

See, you don't have to call a song done forever, you just have to abandon it when your *current* ear is satisfied. You can always come back. The trick is to get something as far as you can take it, then try to take it just a tad further. Then let it go without getting too emotionally involved and start your next tune.

My approach as a producer now isn't to reach some sort of perfection, but to construct something that sounds good to my ears and feels good in my body, arrange it into a full song format, and finally fix the problems.

Some of the issues I find I need to solve are:

- The song sounds muddy, what sound do I need to clean up? Do I need more high frequency content?

- This part has been going on too long without change, how can I retrigger some excitement?

- I seem to have lost the groove, what is taking away from the rhythm?

- Everything seems to be coming from the center, how can I add more movement?

- This sound isn't cutting through, should I add EQ, compression or saturation?

- This new sound is overpowering another important sound, can I solve this with panning or EQ?

The list goes on and on, but you get the idea.

Getting out of the DAW

When I feel I am getting close to completing my song, I will mix it down and listen to the song outside of my DAW. Sometimes visual cues can trick you, so I like to be 100% using my ears.

While listening, I'll make a note of issues with the mix and the time it is happening. This is extremely useful to me, because I know exactly what I need to do to call this song done. I no longer need to overthink, I just go through my checklist.

When there are no more issues I can perceive, I call the song done and move on to the next one.

The most important habit of finishing songs

I want to make it so straight forward and so simple that there is really no way to misunderstand this tip. We have all used this habit to some extent but we don't realize what we are missing when songs aren't getting done any more.

Maybe you feel you've got pretty good studio habits and you are regularly taking time out of your schedule to make writing songs a priority. That is great. If you are there, you are doing better than most, however, how many songs have you *finished*?

If you are like I was, you have a huge pile of unfinished work. They all started off good, but you ran into a glitch. Something wasn't working or you didn't know where to go next. Now there it sits, a never ending 16 bar loop. Don't worry, we've all been there.

I've found one magic bullet that works every time (unless you spontaneously combust in the process). It might not be pretty, but the road to success rarely is.

Pick one

Ok, so here is where you get to make a choice. You have a bunch of unfinished work on your hard drive and you have an idea brewing in your head. Figure out which idea should take priority and get to work. Multitasking rarely works and in most cases will keep you from getting anything completed. Think about it. What have you accomplished that didn't require you to prioritize, focus and work at until it's done?

I know your argument. "What if this song just isn't working?"

Tough shit. You chose it. You finish it. Maybe it will be great and maybe it will suck. Your job is to do the best you can and then let it go. This is a new habit you're building and I'm sure you are quite aware that when you try something new, you are going to suck at it. Although doing your best is a concern, the actual outcome shouldn't be. Here's why...

What you are doing now is not "cranking out hits"... yet. You are building a habit of going up against one frustration after another and getting yourself over the hurdle each time. As you do this process over and over your brain will better be able to problem solve because you will have more experience at dealing with it. Do this ten or twenty times and you'll probably find that what previously was a problem is no longer an issue. Of course, as you get better you will likely give yourself new challenges to face. That's fine, because you will never return to that place you started.

Am I suggesting creative torture?

Not at all when you think about it. What is more painful? The frustration involved in getting over a hurdle, or the regret of letting that hurdle beat you like it beat every other second rate artist?

Chip away at the mountain

I'm not suggesting that you lock yourself in a room and don't eat until you are done with your masterpiece. What I am suggesting is that you choose your song wisely, and take your focus away from every other unfinished idea you have. They can wait. Work on this song consistently. Set aside just 5 minutes every day. Most of the time if you can get yourself started, you'll have the momentum you need to keep going for a while. Perhaps if you can get your 5 minutes done you can commit to another fifteen minutes without distraction. No Facebook or Twitter, just working on your music. Remind yourself that you can take a break or stop after the fifteen minutes is up, or you can recommit to another fifteen minutes.

Try to do this every day. Start with 5 minutes and go from there. If you feel the need to look up techniques, tell yourself you can do it after you've put in the time you've committed to.

The first song might take you a week, or a month. It doesn't matter. The time would have passed anyway, only now you'll have a finished piece of work to show for it. It might not be perfect, but nothing ever is. Learn from it and you'll find the next song goes a little faster, and the one after that, even faster.

Doing it publicly

I've said it before & I'll say it again, it's a good idea to publicly share that you'll be finishing a new song. This way your friends will hold you accountable and give extra motivation to getting it done.

There is no easy way to get good at completing songs, so you might as well choose that first song and get started right away.

The Top 11 causes of Writer's Block and How to break the cycle

Writer's block is a creativity killer that we've all run into time and time again. Sometimes these periods can last days or months. In my case, it was years. Sure, I still toyed around with new programs and made a few decent ideas, but nothing was completed or released during this time.

The sad thing is that it's easy to use writer's block as a crutch so we define every creative obstacle as a form of writer's block and give up. Many of us don't even bother to try to define what writer's block even is. Lack of inspiration? Lack of motivation? A creative black hole?

All of these definitions could be accurate, but let's start calling it by its real name. Fear.

Fear is something you can face and overcome, unlike something as impenetrable as writer's block. Sounds like a disease with no cure but to wait it out doesn't it? It's not.

Let me try to shed some light on the subject, and hopefully set you back on the path of creating right away. Below are habits and belief systems that have lead me to the dreaded writer's block, and some ways to crawl out of that hole.

Avoiding simplicity - A huge obstacle many people have is that they are trying too hard to impress themselves and their peers. Every idea that they come up with seems too obvious, too simple, or both.

It's important to remember though, you are writing a song, not a riff. The only way a song can work is when it lays on top of a simple foundation. When you let go of your ego and just bang out a few chords, you'll find that more complex ideas will come to you as you play those simple parts back.

Complex parts are always derived from a more simplistic idea, so don't be afraid to start simple and add layers until you hear something interesting. If you come up with a better idea later on, you can always scrap your simple parts later. More often than not though, it'll be the simple parts that will give your song its backbone.

Don't over complicate. Start with something you might consider overly simple, obvious or amateur if you have no other inspiration. Keep building the idea until something interesting comes of it. If it doesn't turn into something you love, don't sweat it. You've pushed past the fear of simplicity and survived.

Avoiding sucking - This is a huge one. Anyone is capable of sucking and we don't want to be in that category, so instead we hold out for genius. This can be a very long wait. During this time, you get more and more out of practice, so your current skills start to get rusty. The longer you wait, the harder it is to jump back on that horse.

It's a much better idea to challenge your fear of sucking head on every time. If you can't make genius, make something that sucks just for the hell of it. Have a laugh. Do you have any idea how much genius was created this very way?

Why are you so afraid of sucking? Tell me one thing you are good at now that you weren't worse at when you started? Everyone who has created genius has a lot of suck in their closets that you haven't heard. Don't sweat it. Your job is to choose which of your creations are the best ones to share. Never stop creating altogether because you are afraid of sucking. Anytime you push yourself outside of your comfort zone, you are going to have to face the fear of sucking. Might as well get used to it now instead of later.

No Feedback - This is a big one these days. We create for ourselves, but if we are honest, we also create for the reaction and feedback of others. It's why we got into this.

When all you have to do these days is make a clever post on Facebook to get "liked", this instant gratification becomes a curse when you are writing music. You want to know as you are in the process of writing whether something is good or bad.

The excitement of others fuels the creative process, whether it be friends, bandmates or family (although, your family will rarely tell you your work is genius). It's good to look over your shoulder for some feedback when you are unsure. Not having it can put you in the fearful position of having to think through a creative block on your own, not knowing if you are building on an idea that doesn't have a good foundation to start with.

I hate to be the bearer of bad news, but sometimes you are gonna have to grow some balls and be willing to say "I like this and I'm willing to take the risk that you won't!" To always rely on other people is going to hinder you from finding your own unique way, and *that* is what the world wants from you anyway.

I'm not saying you shouldn't work with other people or get opinions. Just always be prepared to accept criticism and go your own direction anyway. It's liberating.

Creative beliefs - A big part of writer's block is the belief that some people have got *it* and some people don't. What you spend your time doing is figuring out which side of the fence you are on. This is a trap. Nobody can be inspired if they hold the belief that whatever it is that makes someone a true artist, they don't have it.

You are going to have to reprogram your belief system to the understanding that there are some people that persevere through their creative challenges, and those who give up.

It's pretty easy to know which side you stand on with that belief and the remedy is crystal clear. The *it* is something that comes from putting so much time into your craft that you no longer fear it.

Social media - This is really similar to having no feedback in our creative lives. The first thing we want to do when we feel insecure with our creations is make a clever post on your social network of choice. This gives you your "fix" of approval.

The downside is that it becomes so easy to get approval this way that doing real creative work takes a backseat. A good way to break this pattern is to intermix creativity and social media by announcing your creative goals, and putting up your progress for those who support you.

It's really important to create partnerships with other musicians of a similar vibe or style. These are your "go to" people when you want feedback on an idea.

Get yourself a Soundcloud page, and post private links to people you trust to be the most constructive and honest. You may also want to make a separate page on your Facebook or Google+ strictly for your music. If you are going to be on those sites, you might as well use them to build your support team.

Brand yourself as an artist so people will expect work from you. This should help break the pattern of instant gratification. Also, never forget that you are in the driver's seat. You can ask for directions, but never hand over your car.

Tutorials - It may seem taboo for a guy who makes tutorials to say this, but I think it's important to realize that tutorials alone aren't likely to build your song writing confidence. In fact, if you aren't putting what you learn immediately to use, these tutorials likely won't do you much good. If you only consume information and don't put it to use, you'll lose the habit and motivation to write. Then you'll become afraid to write, and that's exactly what writer's block is.

Sometimes watching people way above your skill level can inspire you, but other times it can make you feel unqualified and unprepared to make music.

Don't let yourself fall into this trap. Put on a Sex Pistols album and rebuild your confidence by making something within your current skill levels.

I personally like albums made by less talented musicians, because I feel like I can hear that angst in the music of not being able to fully express themselves. Have you ever read somebody writing about something that affected them so much that they struggled to find the words? That is powerful and should be embraced.

I don't mean you should lower your standards. Instead, accept that the genius isn't in the complexity of things. It's in looking at simplicity from a different angle and layering these simple ideas to build something new.

Too many choices

When I started using drum machines, samplers and synths, the options were exciting, but it took ages to choose a sound palette. By the time I got ideas laid down, I had forgotten the original inspiration, leaving me with an uninspired set of sounds.

I'm not blaming the machines. I'm blaming myself for not having the foresight to know my own sound and search for those few patches that sounded like *me*.

I encourage you to take the time to build some *go to* sound patches, drum kits, etc. These are patches that already sound good and inspiring to you. These should be the first sounds you go to when starting a new track (a guitar or piano is also a great place to start). This way you can bang out something that sounds good as the ideas come to you.

You can always change things later, but you'll have the advantage of solid ideas to give you direction when exploring unfamiliar sounds, synths, samples etc.

If you want to bust your writers block, have good sounds ready at all times or your favorite instrument at arm's reach. Would you be surprised to know that Vince Clarke (*Depeche Mode/Yaz/Erasure*) starts all his songs on guitar? He saves all the noodling on synths til after he knows he's got a song worth writing. Something to keep in mind.

Past failures - So you write a song or a few songs you are excited about and the reaction you get it less than enthusiastic. This one is tough. I've been there myself. After sharing this music you've worked hard on, your motivation to continue making music is shattered and writer's block sets in.

The thing you need to realize is that everyone does stuff that isn't up to par.

Everyone.

Secondly, your friends will rarely share your excitement. Sometimes they just aren't into your style. If you aren't directly copying another artist, you're likely to come across people who just don't *get* it. People tend to praise the familiar, so if you're getting a lot of praise from people close to you, be cautious. You might not be very original.

Now let's say this person who isn't into your stuff has a point. Have you exercised that constructive criticism muscle lately? It's time you start.

Here's what is great about constructive (or even critical) criticism. When you are put in a situation where you have to defend your work, you are putting your conviction to the test.

The people who challenge your work are the only ones who will give you an opportunity to defend it. Most likely, you'll discover the parts of your work that you are most proud of because the criticism won't bother you as much. It's the stuff you aren't as confident in that really bites you in the ass. To hear someone point out these things is just confirming what you already know, you're not quite there.

Would you prefer to release something that is substandard because no one challenged your work? Every major artist who works with an engineer will hear "maybe not so much of that, it's not really working". That's what they are hired for (I think George Lucas could have used more of them with his last few movies).

To have past failures doesn't mean you suck, it just means you haven't written enough music. You should look forward to criticism, it's a form of quality control that *every* artist needs. We aren't talking about perfection here, we are just trying to get it to a higher quality standard. In the end, perfection doesn't end up sounding good anyway. It's like quantizing everything you do

100% to a 1/16th note grid. Life=gone. Imperfection gives life to your music and art.

Past successes - This can be even worse than past failures, and is something I've had to deal with myself. After having some success with my tracks in the progressive house field, it first made me question what I was doing right and how to repeat it. Then my ability to write was hindered by the fear that my new tracks would sound amateur and ruin the reputation I had built. This led to literally years of not finishing tracks.

It took a lot to get myself back in the game, and by that time I had lost some of my chops and the tracks weren't as well received. Now I realize that had I not stopped, the quality of work would have likely been better, but even if it wasn't, I'd get over that hump and on to new tunes soon enough. It's a hard lesson that I hope you don't have to go through.

When you have success, take note of what you did well but move on and do something new quickly. Don't sit too long feeling good about yourself or you'll become crippled and not able to move. Try to ignore the fact that you were well received, and just keep making music you like and have fun making it.

There are bands that have made brilliant albums later in their career that will always be known for one hit song early on. *Radiohead* – "Creep" for example. Just imagine what a loss it would be for music if they stopped after their first album. They did the right thing by pushing outside their comfort zone. "Creep" might be their most popular song but I certainly wouldn't consider it close to their best or even the sound their true fans know them for.

Don't stop writing, don't get too comfortable and don't conform for success. It could be the end of you if you do.

Chasing your tail - So many musicians are searching for a shortcut. That one tune that will change everything. So instead of listening to their own creative intuition, they are constantly searching for friends, charts, radio and TV to tell them what they should be doing.

The problem with this of course is that it's very rare to build a career by doing what is currently popular. By the time you finish your perfect dubstep album, the trend is over-saturated and played out and of course, since you were putting your focus into following trends, you lost your ability to have confidence in your own ideas. Now *that* style is toast and you look for another trend to follow.

This habit will likely get you nowhere, and you'll likely never build your own sound. Your new goal will be to make songs that sound like songs other people have already made so that your friends will respect you.

Now I have no problem with being a fan boy of some sort. It's pretty much how we all start. We hear something we connect with and think "I want to do *that!*"

Fair enough. Just make sure you are ready for the long haul and that you are injecting other influences that excite *you*, not what you think others will like. It would be hard for me to think of a more sure way to give yourself writer's block than trying to please others.

Want to break this habit real quick?

Write something you like that you expect your friends won't. Do it on purpose just to freak them out. Don't purposely make a song that sucks, just pick an influence of yours that is less popular and have fun with it. Stop asking what others would do, and start asking "What would I do?" It might not be your best work, but it is incredibly liberating. And who knows, maybe your friends will end up liking it anyway.

Gear envy

You've got this amazing song idea in your head, but you don't want to start it 'til you get that new gadget. You saw someone going apeshit with it on YouTube and you now consider it the Holy Grail. *This* is exactly why your music hasn't been up to par!

You get it home, love it for a month (but never actually make a song with it), and then you're back to YouTube looking for another piece of kit, sample cd, soft synth, plugin or whatever.

Stop!

All you are going to do is spend a lot of money, have some bragging rights, but never get anything done. You, my friend, have become a gear hoarder (they will soon make TV shows about you). Plus you haven't even learned what your current tools are capable of.

I promise you, you can write a great tune with what you have now. Let's be honest. Think of the best tune you ever wrote (or the best unfinished idea, if you aren't there yet). Was it the gear that made it great? Are your newest tracks with your latest toys always your best? I'm willing to bet there is something else. Something not so tangible that makes it good.

It can be maddening to see these popular musicians with shitloads of gear filling up their studio, but I guarantee what got them there wasn't the gear. It was good ideas and doing the best with what they had. Even *U2* started small, and some people would argue that their best albums were before they had every toy known to man. Luckily, they aren't hindered by the gear. At the end of the day it's a guitarist, bassist, drummer and singer jamming things out that makes good songs.

If lack of gear is giving you writers block, then just tell yourself you are making a demo with what you have now and will it improve later. I think you'll be impressed with your results. Any result is better than no results.

Writer's block is simply fear disguised as other things. It's certainly not something that is out of your control. Make creating a habit, even if it's for fifteen minutes a day. Whatever you do, never stop because of fear.

12 ways to triple your productivity and make more music

In all honesty, I'm naturally a pretty lazy guy. At times I sleep too much, fill up my time with nonsense and completely close off to creative endeavors. All that I have accomplished has been in the face of heavy motivational challenges. Believe me when I say that if you are running into motivational issues, I've certainly been there.

These tips below are discoveries I have made to battle my own laziness, fatigue and creative anxiety. I have found that when I follow these guidelines and resist bad habits, I'm not only far more productive, but I have a much greater sense of peace and relaxation overall. Give it a shot!

1. **Warm up.** Just like you would with a workout, it's really difficult to dive right in to creative work from whatever you were doing previously. You'll likely resist because it will just feel *wrong* to you. You'll feel that there is something else important that needs to be done even if you can't pinpoint what that is. When you already have non-productive momentum, it's hard to turn that boat around.

   Take a break first. Take a fifteen minute walk or do some light exercise. You want to create a gap between what you were doing before and what you are attempting to do creatively. You need a bit of time to clean the slate, so your head isn't filled up with a bunch of crap.

2. **Don't check email or social sites.** This one is a tough habit to break but it's one you are really going to need to commit to if you are planning to be more productive. Social sites and email make it far too easy to convince yourself that you need to stay unproductive just in case something happens. Maybe someone will "like" your post, comment or picture, or maybe you've started a debate with some idiot on YouTube and need to set him straight.

Face it, it's all bullshit, and if you keep at it your life is going to waste away. The thing that is really sad about this is that the brain gets a rush of adrenaline every time you get a notification, even if it's something stupid and *this* is how you get a feeling of accomplishment for doing nothing. Then when it comes to doing "real" work you feel like your plate has already been filled, and you have no room for any more "productivity". Days turn into months... then years.

Stop it! If you really want to get WAY more done, cut your social network checking to two-three times a day, and only *after* you've put in some real creative work.

3. **Identify your creative blind spots.** We all have them. They are the things that stop us from completing songs. It's those things we naturally aren't good at. For me, it was sound design and song arrangement. I would make 16 bar loops with ease, but after that I start itching to check my email and then all is lost. We'll solve this issue with my next tip.

4. **Steal then replace.** If you are running into a similar issue to what was just mentioned, my suggestion is to just nick that sound or song structure from something you already know works. Don't try to reinvent the wheel. Steal it first and move on. You can always replace it later, but the goal is to not get stuck and slow down (or worse, stop). I nick sounds or song structures all the time. It really helps me with my confidence knowing that what I am "borrowing" is already something that works. I don't have to second guess.

Often, for me, my own voice will eventually peek through and I'll abandon my borrowed templates or sounds and go it alone once again. Keep practicing this habit and you'll find it gets easier and easier. Soon you'll have the confidence to push through without getting stuck or needing to snag a sound or template. (By the way, if sampling is your style, carry on. I'm a big fan of those who do it well)

5. **Set a timer**. This tip alone has been a saving grace for me. I typically start with setting a fifteen minute timer to warm up for the task ahead. I try to avoid doing anything that can suck me in to further mindless activity. I make sure what I am doing is relaxing, and isn't actually going to take longer than I've set the timer for.

Once the timer goes off, it's time to commit to making music (or writing this book) and set the timer once again. This time I set it to thirty minutes and make a commitment to stay off the internet, not responding to texts or phone calls and making sure people in my house don't interrupt me.

The reason this works so well is because even if you really don't want to create, you can tell yourself "It's only thirty minutes, then I can choose to do something else if I want." Once the timer goes off I can decide if I want to recommit to another thirty minutes, take a fifteen minute break and come back, or call it a day. I typically will recommit, however if I get stuck, I give myself fifteen minutes to search for inspiration.

Sometimes I'll break song writing down to different tasks. This way I can actually see progress happening every time I recommit. For the most recent project I did as of writing this, I was creating a song from a bunch of random loops sent to me by my lovely readers. It was tricky to get my head around how I was going to construct a song out of all the pieces so I started committing to small tasks:

- Edit and effect each loop for my own purposes

- Create different possible sections or "movements" for this song.

- Find a song structure to "borrow" and map it out using locator tags.

- Construct a 32 bar intro

- Bridge the gap between each section for a transparent sound that also makes sense.

- Create an Outro

- Final mixing tweaks and rendering a mix down.

Some tasks took longer than others, but when I noticed progress in any of the song writing stages I usually had enough momentum built up to continue for another thirty minutes, and then another.

Also, make sure if you're looking for inspiration to get over the next hurdle, that you set a timer for that, otherwise you're likely to completely derail. Knowing that you've only got fifteen minutes to figure something out will keep you more focused on things you'll be able to put to use right away.

6. **One task at a time.** This simple tip gets overlooked far too often, especially in this age of ADHD and multitasking. I can say however, with very few exceptions that taking on one thing at a time until it's completed is really the fastest and most productive way.

The alternative will leave you with several unfinished tasks that you worked on up to the point where things got difficult. Then you'll find yourself completely unmotivated to finish any of these tasks, because you haven't built up the discipline to work through the tough parts. Had you committed to one task at a time, you would have worked through the roadblocks that sets you apart from your peers and competitors. You will also have built the momentum to take on your next task.

Let's take this book for example. If I didn't commit myself, I'd have nothing but unfinished notes. Same with music. I know this because I used to have a serious habit of leaving songs unfinished, and going long periods without sharing any new music.

At times I might be in the middle of one song when another song idea jumps in my head. When that happens, I'll usually set aside a small amount of time to document the idea so it's not forgotten, but I'll set a timer so I don't get off track from my main focus.

Give this a serious try and I dare you to tell me you aren't far more productive.

7. **Write down your creative tasks the night before**. This really helps your brain prepare to for the tasks of the following day and do some problem solving while you sleep. You may have the issue that I've often had where making music just doesn't seem like what you should be doing when you haven't been in the habit for a while. It's really similar to trying to motivate yourself to start exercising when you're out of shape. Writing down a few tasks to complete the night before helps to solve this, as well as making the process go more smoothly.

8. **Pretend you know how**. There is no issue with learning techniques from experts. I can definitely say I have learned some things I probably would have never come across myself, but had I not explored things on my own, I would never have become more than an imitator. Instead of spending hours upon hours scouring the internet, books and magazines to solve all of your challenges, try believing in your own abilities and resourcefulness. The more you do this, the better you get at it. Soon you'll find that you aren't simply an expert at imitating, but you'll be coming up with innovative ideas and further refining your own sound. You'll be surprised how much you actually *do* know.

9. **Blueprint first, details later**. Don't get caught up for hours trying to perfect that snare drum when you don't even have a song structure yet. You'll likely need to further tweak it later anyway. Instead focus on the broad strokes. Work on the essential musical elements and then a basic song structure, before agonizing over whether something sounds better 1/2 a dB louder or quieter. Having a basic sketch complete makes it much easier to see the big picture while dialing in the little details.

10. **Start creating before setting other tasks**. If your goal is to make (and finish) music you can be proud of, instead of

going another year with very little creative output, making music should be on your "essential" list. If you prioritize other tasks during your free time, you have little chance of your music taking center stage. If you simply can't do this most of the time, at least make music a top priority one day out of the week. If you can't make time now, when do you expect your schedule will open up? Trust me, it won't!

11. **Take breaks often**. If you are on a roll, go with it. Being in the flow is a very enjoyable experience and there is no reason to disrupt that. It's more common, however, to lose steam on a project within 90 minutes than it is to find yourself in marathon mode. Make sure to give yourself a short break every hour to 90 minutes. This is supposed to be pleasant after all. Also your ears need a break too, or they won't be reliable. A break is a small reward for a job well done. Knowing you'll get a break soon will push you to work harder and stay focused. Those of you who've read *The Shining* should know that "all work and no play makes Jack a dull boy". Don't be Jack.

12. **Commit publicly**. There is not much better motivation than having your peers expecting something you have promised to deliver. If you aren't willing to make this promise publicly, then maybe you don't have enough belief in yourself to get past the roadblocks that make most people quit.

I personally use this technique to take on challenges that scare me because I know that otherwise, the likelihood of me accomplishing these tasks is pretty slim. I used this technique to create my 30 Day Music Production Journal. I allowed myself to be embarrassed publicly to make certain fear doesn't rule my life.

I hope you find a way to put some or all of these tips to use.

Secrets to holding a listeners attention

The challenge many of us have when making songs based on either premade or self-made loops of one, two, four or eight bars is that it can be difficult to keeps things sounding interesting and exciting. I run into this scenario quite a bit, and I'd like to share some tip sand ideas to help you improve the flow and interest of your tracks.

Filters

Filters and resonance is probably the most obvious way to keep interest in a part that loops. Closing a hi pass filter can create a feeling of tension or repressed energy, and opening the filter creates a nice release. Depending on the part, this can be very intentional and noticeable, or subtle. Either way it can keep the listeners attention, as the ears are impeccable at distinguishing minor changes and fluctuations. Two or three builds in your song can go a long way to keep your track interesting.

Lfo's

An LFO (or Low frequency oscillator) is a fantastic way to create subtle movement in your loop or midi part. If you are working with a synth, adding an *lfo* to volume, panning, filter or pitch is usually possible directly on your hardware or soft synth. It doesn't take much to give a sound more life. Sometimes you can't really notice exactly what is happening with your sound, but you just instinctively know that it sounds more interesting. If you are working with a sampled loop, you may need to add an effect that offers *lfo* movement. Adding something as simple as a *chorus* or *flanger* at a low "wet" percentage can really help. For more randomness I wouldn't sync the *lfo* to tempo. A slow *lfo* that repeats out of sync with the tempo will keep the *lfo's* themselves from being too loopy.

Duplicate and Layer

I use this technique a lot. There are one of a few things I might do to keep things interesting. I will duplicate my loop and make the duplicate an octave higher or lower to introduce different frequency information. Often times I'll go an octave higher and filter out most of the low frequency content so it doesn't clash with the original part or other parts in the song. Then I'll add some dirt with a type of distortion or saturator. Next I'll automate the volume subtly so hints of it comes in and out of the mix. I may make it more noticeable during breakdowns and buildups. You can also add a layer that is a harmonic of the original. I like trying to re-pitch a duplicated layer 5 or 7 semitones above the original. See what works for you.

Also something to look into is duplicating your part and reversing it. Then find the parts that sound interesting, cut them up, and strategically place them in interesting places. It will often assist, and enhance the feel and movement of the loop if not overdone.

Send/Returns

This can be similar to the last tip. You would simply create interesting FX chains on several return tracks. One might use *bit reduction* and *erosion*. Another might introduce an interesting *delay* or *reverb*, while another has a *chorus* or *phaser*. It's best to put the wet/dry on 100%(on the return track), as you don't want to send the original track back into itself in most cases. Once you have those chains, each of your tracks, including your loop track will have send knobs in your session view. Your track sends are just as automate-able as *volume* or *panning*, so automate subtle hints of each effect in different points of your song. This is certain to keep things interesting. Just make sure not to get lost here. You were probably attracted to the original loop for a reason, so make sure you aren't diluting what makes the part great.

Attack, decay, and release times

This is another technique that can make a huge impact on your synth part. Unfortunately, you won't have this option with a sampled loop, but I'll give you a tip that might still help. If you are using a synth, you are sure to have *attack, decay, sustain* and *release*. In most cases, I like to back off my sustain and release to the lowest setting, and then tweak the decay between long and short times. It's great to open the decay up during builds and breaks, and then back it off when things kick back in. This can bring your sound from choppy to washy. Experimenting with the attack can create interesting results at times too. Just like I said before, make sure you don't lose perspective of the loop that inspired you in the first place. If you are working with a sample, you can drag in a *gate* effect and experiment with the threshold. Sometimes this can create a similar effect.

Sidechaining

This is a dance producer's secret weapon and can easily be overused, but the movement and groove it can give a part can't be denied. Subtly (or more noticeably) syncing a loop to the kick can certainly help keep things interesting. Naturally when the kicks drop out, so does the sidechain effect which has been pretty popular in dance music. Whether you choose a standard noticeable approach or something more subtle, the listeners' ears will thank you. Also experiment with side chaining to other parts in your song for interesting results.

Outside the loop

Although there are many things you can do to make a repeating loop sound interesting, there is also something to be said about building interest outside the loop. In general, the listener is not going to want to hear a static loop for more than 8 bars. There are things outside the loop that obviously need to stay interesting as well. Filter rises, swells, evolving ambient sounds and high frequency sounds are some of my favorite ways to keep interest.

Many songs, for example, will put a crash or impact sound at every 8 to 16 bars. Surprisingly, that one sound can reset your interest in listening to a loop for another 8 to 16 bars (depending on how interesting the loop itself is). On top of that though, reverse sounds and weird noises run through reverb and delay can really create space and depth in your track.

Another favorite trick of mine is stretching audio. Whether it be a vocal sample or, well, pretty much anything, you can really get some amazing drones with tons of subtle movement. Heck, even try stretching your loop itself. I prefer using a fantastic free program called *Paul Stretch*. It does some fantastic things and can bring endless fun!

I know there are ways to keep a track free from too many effects and dry sounding without losing interest as well, and that would have a lot to do with drum programming, groove quantizing and knowing when to add another layer of hi-hats or when to drop the kick for dramatic effect. Hip Hop is really good at this, but remember, most hip hop is only a few minutes long and has vocals throughout. Getting the same results on a 7 minute track without vocals is much more challenging. I'm certainly not an authority on this approach, but I admire those who are able to take a minimal approach and keep things interesting and engaging.

Other things to note for keeping interest are counter melodies. Being able to change the attention from one melody to another can keep listener interest for a far longer time. Just make sure both parts have movement and have areas in the song where each is more noticeable than the other as well as a part where both parts are layered pretty evenly. That alone gives you three movements for your track.

Last but not least, changing just one note in your bassline can make a dramatic effect if done in the right place. Don't underestimate the power the bass plays on a melodic loop. Changing the key of your bass, or just a note here and there can do wonders to keep interest.

Use your best judgement

All of these techniques are simply suggestions, and it's really going to come down to your personal style and what you would like to accomplish. Some techniques might not benefit your track at all, or perhaps you've found the perfect loop that needs very little to keep interesting. You are the master of your own craft, and ultimately, you make the rules. All I am hoping to do is empower you to be the best YOU possible.

Creating Evolving Loops/Soundscapes

This is a simple way to take one boring midi loop and make it much more interesting through layering the same part through different effects chains. I also show you a trick of creating automation for each layer that loops at odd times. If you think of running several tape loops all at different lengths, when played together, the sounds never combine the same way twice. This makes things more pleasing and interesting to the ears.

Essentials when making tracks for the Dancefloor

When it comes to writing electronic music for clubs, it's often a good idea to have a few things in mind before you tackle that track.

- Who is this track for?

- What DJ's would I want playing this song?

- What should I use as a reference to keep me on track?

Although plagiarism is most likely going to make you look like a sad imitator, not knowing the proper structure and elements that make a track in a certain style work can also make you look pretty amateur.

Templates

For me, it's not about plagiarism or theft (unless you consider any type of sampling to be theft), it's about understanding the template before you randomly bang out a few loops and expect a dancefloor *hit* to result. It's like knowing which colors complement each other on canvas to get a certain result. As much as we would like to take credit for being the sole influence of every great piece of work we've done, every style of music has a template.

Breaking rules can be pretty important in expanding a sound and pushing boundaries, but push too far and you're either in another subgenre of music or your song gives the impression that it has somehow missed the mark. This can be that either too much is going on, not enough is going on, or that the structure leaves you feeling bored or overstimulated.

In business they say that if you want to be successful, you should model someone who is already successful in your field. I think the same goes for music.

For me, I'd be a bit like a train without a track without some sort of template. I usually don't have a template when I am jamming ideas, but once I get into arrangement and mixing mode, I definitely have a reference, format or template in mind.

Usually I let templates assist me when it comes to figuring out the elements I need for a complete track. Without having something to reference, I can easily fill the song with too much in one area and not enough in another area. So I may listen to a track for guidance, even if it's one of my own completed songs. I'll map out the elements something like this:

- Kick

- Drums

- Percussion

- Crash

- Drone

- Bass

- Pads

- Lead or hook

- Cut up bits

- "Build up" sounds

- FX

This, of course, is a very basic list off the top of my head, but it's good enough for this example. With these, I take a loose mental note of the basic frequency ranges of each part. This can expose holes in my frequency spectrum, and lead me to know if I need to play that pad an octave higher or lower etc.

It's important to not try to fill up all the frequencies at all times. Without some gaps, it'll be difficult to build excitement. It's important to know how few elements the track can run on and stay sonically interesting. Leaving a hole in the high frequencies, for example, can make room for those hi hats that come in on the offbeat at certain peak points in the track.

Given these elements above, I would make sure that each part in my song either fell directly into one of these categories, or was playing a necessary support role to one of these elements. A bass, for example, might need three elements working together to get the right sound. Typically, each layer will consist of a different frequency range which, when put together, make one rich dynamic sound.

If you are playing three different parts in the same bass frequency, you're most likely going to want to either cut something, or re-EQ one of the parts so they don't interfere with each other. Interference causes a lack of clarity, and the overall impact is likely to suffer.

DJ mixes vs songs

When it comes to building a template of sounds I prefer to listen to a live DJ mix, instead of individual songs. There are a few reasons for this.

For one, you are able to find common themes and patterns in the overall sound of the mix, instead of taking direct influence from one artist alone. You are also able to hear the elements of the songs that are being highlighted in the mix, and which are not being used.

It may turn out that a DJ needs to re-edit or layer a track for it to work on the dancefloor. If you are able to listen to a four+ hour mix, you can really get an idea of how the DJ builds his set in a live situation, instead of the snapshot that is given on a commercial DJ mix CD.

This also gives you the ability to know whether your style is best suited for the early, mid or late portion of a set. Where individual tracks come in handy is when looking for inspiration in the arrangement of your song.

Ask a DJ

Most DJ's I share my music with gives great feedback. It's pretty normal for any producer to have their songs "road tested" before they settle on a final mix. If you have a friend that DJ's in well-established clubs around the world, you'll be doing yourself a huge favor by listening to what they have to say. This, of course, is assuming they play the kind of music you make.

Writing music for the public can be pretty scary. Putting something out into the world is your way of saying "I think this is good and I'm gambling my reputation on it." Don't let that scare you off though, every artist is going through the same thing, so you're in very good company.

Evolution Music Production

Haven't heard of Evolution Production? Either had I.

But since starting the *One Hour a Day Ableton Group* I've come to make several new discoveries when it comes to music making. These discoveries have increased my music output by probably 1000% with no exaggeration at all.

Evolution Production is a term I coined for a process that has given me some pretty incredible results. Let me explain.

One of the absolute worst things a creative person can face is a blank page, a blank canvas or in our case, a blank computer screen. In fact, I'd go so far as to say we hate it so much that we will unconsciously sabotage ourselves into not finishing our music for fear of facing the mountain all over again.

For computer musicians who are trying to improve their skills, this can be a huge energy drain. You've just finished a track that took loads of time & effort & now have the pressure of building something completely new, that requires a new template of sounds and tools.

Although all experience is good experience, you aren't practicing one skill long enough to get proficient at it. Instead, you convince yourself you are bored, abandon your current skill set and go after that shiny new sound that peaks your interest. That is, if you can even find the motivation to get started.

This is similar to being a science fiction writer and before getting proficient at that skill, writing horror, then a mystery and perhaps a documentary next. Unfortunately, we creatives tend to repeatedly change direction or set a new goal before we ever "nail" the last one.

You know what they say about the jack of all trades. He's not very good at any of them.

The Evolution approach

Everybody knows practice makes perfect. What they don't tell you (although it should be obvious to most of us), is that you have to practice the same actions repeatedly until it becomes second nature. As you do this, you make little tweaks that, over time, dramatically improve your results.

Here's a tool that not only will greatly increase your creative output, but you will also notice you are continuously getting better and fine tuning your skills into creative *crack*.

1. The first step, *and this is an important one*, is to choose your direction for the long term. You are going to stick with it until you excel at it, so don't pick something that is just going to be a passing interest for you, really think about how you want to define yourself as an artist for the next year.

2. If you have any unfinished ideas that are in this direction, it'll be easier for you to get started, because you won't be starting with a blank slate. If you don't have something to get you started, collect some songs that have the vibe you are looking for, or better yet, a DJ mix since it'll be a more cohesive sound. Work on building a template with drum sounds, bass and signature sounds that will get you started. I know this is the hard part, but you'll really only have to do it once.

3. Having your sounds *at the ready* is extremely important if you want to have a solid workflow. You don't want to mess around searching for sounds when you are trying to make music. It's ok if the sounds aren't perfect. Just make sure they are inspiring enough to get you moving.

4. Start building a groove that fits your style, get enough going on that your song sounds legit for at least 32 bars. Dial in your sounds with EQ, compression and effects that give you what you are looking for.

5. Before going into full arrangement mode save your tune. Then Copy & paste 4-8 bars of your loop & past it to an empty section of your arrangement window. Mute anything that is key specific (so you don't have key clashing) and write a new bassline, or if you prefer, a new melody (or both) using the sounds you have already just created. Save this as another tune that you can open after you have finished your current song. Now you know you won't have a blank slate when starting the next song and will be able to build something new quickly.

6. When you start dialing in your new song, you will likely tweak or improve your current sounds and make small improvements to your template and change how the beats play or even the tempo. Once you get the next groove dialed in for 32 bars, repeat step 5. This way, as you are getting better at dialing in the sounds you want and improving your skill set, you've always got your next tune idea ready to go. Your skills will evolve & improve with each new project.

Simple right?

I've found myself having loads of basslines in my head recently or having a sample or two that I want to put to use, so instead of building up from scratch, I piggyback on my previous work, to get the idea out quickly. Sometimes during one song session I'll have three new ideas that spark from it. It only takes me fifteen minutes or so to get the new idea out and saved so I can continue finishing my current song.

Using this technique I've been able to finish the better part of 5 tracks within a couple weeks and have several more grooves ready when I am done with those. This is highly motivating and huge in developing your own sound.

Another reason this works so well is because most of your best ideas are sparked when you are already creating. It's like the gods of creativity smile upon you when instead of waiting for inspiration, you just get your ass to work.

When you try it for yourself, you'll realize that each song will take on its own life and end up sounding quite a bit different from the last. Also your template will go through so many evolutions, you will end up with many different starting points to choose from. As long as you are continuing to listen to music and letting new sounds inspire you, there is really no limit to how long you can carry on this process, and how much better you will get at producing in a short amount of time.

Feel free to follow me and several other producers taking on my One Hour a Day Ableton Group Challenge. It's a free group and you are welcome to join in the conversation, or take on the challenge yourself. I've got my daily process for over 50 songs as of writing this. Use this Link: bit.ly/39rj2YQ

Finding the right sounds for your music

I was asked recently in an email:

"How do you know which sounds to use that will complement the other sounds in your song?"

I thought this was a very good question, as I've struggled with this very same issue in the past and I'm sure many of you may have been challenged by this as well.

There seems to be two schools of thought when making music:

1. The rule followers

2. The rule breakers

I always liked to identify with #2, and it gave me loads of freedom as a guitarist & I thought this approach would translate well with electronic music as well, but it didn't and I couldn't figure out why.

Why did every idea seem to fit so well together with the more traditional band format (Guitar, Bass, Drums, Vox and Synth), while my early electronic music projects struggled?

Then it finally clicked.

The songs I made with a standard live instrument set up used pretty much the same instruments, putting out slight variations of the same sound. Each instrument, regardless of what was played, essentially stayed in its own frequency range, leaving room for the other instruments.

Although drums can be pretty complex, frequency-wise each drum sound tends to take up a small part of the spectrum and is not constant. Plus, the sounds have a pretty sharp attack that help them cut through a mix. As long as each musician knows when to back off their instrument a little to make room for other parts at times, the song has a pretty good chance of gelling together nicely with a professional mix.

Let's take a basic look at frequencies for a rock band. These will be pretty general, just to make my point. Although each instrument can have a wider frequency range, I'm going to point out some of the frequencies that are prominent. If you want to argue these, please don't. I'm talking in generalizations here:

- Kick Drum – 50 - 100 Hz with a snap around 1 - 3 kHz

- Snare – 600 Hz - 3 kHz

- Guitar – 650 Hz - 8 kHz

- Vocals – 500 Hz - 7 kHz

- Hi-hats – 8 - 20 kHz

So, if we take a look at these frequencies, we can see that although the vocals and guitars overlap in frequency, everything generally has its space to breathe and be heard. Once a band has dialed in their sound, they can usually hit that frequency pocket fairly easily.

Not so much with electronic music.

Although electronic music does have certain standards that need attention paid to, the new producer doesn't naturally have these instincts. Since there are literally millions of sounds to choose from, the new producer typically stops on any sound that sounds great on its own and makes a riff, then another sound and then another; not keeping in mind that each sound has a frequency range, and that there isn't room for multiple sounds in the same frequency playing at the same time.

Another issue is that people's ears tend to perk up at a specific frequency (usually mids to upper mids) while other frequencies sound dull. If you solo any instrument, you'll tend to think it sounds better when you boost the mids. The problem is that when played with other parts that have all been boosted in the mids, you're going to have a mess. You are also going to have wide gaps of frequencies that aren't being properly represented, making a very thin sounding mix.

The better approach

Think of each sound in your electronic composition as filling a space in the frequency range, like a rock band might. Sure you have different sounds representing each frequency range, but as long as you keep aware of what job each sound is playing in the overall frequency spectrum, you won't be overloading one frequency while neglecting another.

More means less

When it comes to electronic music (hell, any music for that matter, but I digress), there are far fewer rules about how many instruments are the right amount for a complete song. Just understand that the more sounds you have, the thinner the frequency range each sound should be taking up. If you find that two sounds are masking each other because they are fighting for the same frequency, try pitching one of the sounds up or down an octave to see if it fits better in that range.

Remember, if you want a ginormous saw wave bass with a huge frequency range, you better strip down what else you put in this composition, or you'll just end up with a bunch of mud and the bass will suffer.

If you absolutely think two sounds in the same frequency both need to stay in your song, you can do a couple of things.

First, pan each part to a different place in the stereo field. This can often solve simple issues without too much fuss, but it certainly isn't a "fix all".

Second, sweep the frequency range with an EQ until you find the frequency that makes the sound most clear. This is done by boosting a fairly narrow frequency band and running it through the full spectrum of frequencies. When you find that perfect frequency, lower the gain to around +1-2 dB, then reduce the other instrument's EQ in the same frequency by 2-6 dB (or lower if it doesn't negatively affect the overall sound when these parts are played together.

The right sounds

Now that we understand how frequency plays a huge role in your productions, let's get into which sounds are right for your style of music. I said earlier that I considered myself more of a rule breaker than a rule follower, but as I dive into certain electronic niches, I find I am more satisfied with my results when I understand the genre I'm writing inside and out. If your goal is simply to be avant-garde and undefinable, this may not apply to you, yet I still think you'll be able to take something away from it.

For me, this has meant not only listening to relevant songs on Beatport and Soundcloud, but also going to clubs that are known for that style of music, and taking note of what sounds and rhythms move me, what tones create tension, and what tones give that release. Which sounds and rhythms keep occurring throughout the night to great effect, and which get old quickly. This works best when you stick to one genre at a time until you've really internalized it.

I like to use descriptive words for sounds and patterns I like. I like to use words that describe more of the purpose of the sound instead of being too literal. This way, when I pull out my notes when writing, I still have some flexibility of how I can fill that purpose in my own songs. Sometimes I even record parts on my iPhone to reference later, especially if there is a familiar tone or rhythm that is a kind of *blueprint* for the style of music I am wanting to make.

Make your own rules:

Once I have found what I like within the frame of what works in a certain genre, I start to make my own list of "rules" to follow in order to keep me focused and on track. This especially helps if you are the type of person who likes a bit of everything, and tends to go on unfocused tangents.

I might use descriptions like this to describe some of the sounds I am enjoying lately:

- A constant drone for atmosphere and tension
- Sharp overdriven percussion that hits the ears in a pleasing frequency
- Sub bass that is more felt than heard
- Fat dirty kick that sits perfect with the bass and drives the song
- Dirty Clap on the two's and four's
- Hypnotic hi-hat shuffle that isn't too complex - add and subtract reverb to add tension
- Simple Stab rhythm that is percussive and plays 1-3 notes tops
- Filters and swishes for movement, but nothing too over the top
- Classic snare fills and patterns, stick with a familiar and nostalgic vibe
- Filtering the bass in and out to create breaks
- Incidental FX sounds and reverse sounds to keep interest

With this list, I have made some of my own song writing rules to make sure I am using the right sounds and rhythms when I make this type of track. Even with these rules, it still leaves things open wide for experimentation. Also, once you know the rules, you can break them more successfully.

In the same way that you can make a million different songs with the same drum beat or chord structure, I think that even when it comes to following rules, there are endless ways to explore that style of music.

I'm sure your "rules" will vary quite widely from mine. That's perfectly ok of course. I encourage you to develop your sound from your own preferences, not mine or anybody else's.

Save your pre-sets

Each sound you make is going to take you some time to get *right*, even after you know what you want. That's just part of any type of creating. So when you *do* nail that sound, don't forget to save pre-sets that you can use later. It's so much easier to tweak the right sound a bit, than to start from scratch every time you make a new song. Soon you'll have a template of "go to" sounds to get you started easily. That's where the fun really starts!

Create with confidence

Remember that at the end of the day, you will get closer and closer to your sound with practice. Don't spend too much time preparing to write music. Get to it ASAP and be confident that you are improving every time you sit down to create. Just aim to get 1% closer to your goals each day and you'll find yourself improving by leaps and bounds.

Ghost Tracks

When you come to your studio with a blank slate, it can sometimes be difficult to decide what exactly you are going to do. There are several conscious or unconscious questions that will need to be answered.

- What style of music will I be making?

- What tempo will the song be at?

- What key will this song be in?

- What mood would I like to capture?

Sometimes when you are inspired, all of these questions are naturally answered without any trouble, but without that spark of inspiration you are kind of wandering aimlessly hoping that some of your toying around with sounds or rhythms grabs your interest. This can be a long process or can end up with several false starts. A ghost track can be the solution.

What is a ghost track?

The process of a ghost track is very simple. Typically you find a song that affects you on an emotional level. Something that captures a mood and inspires you. You don't have to know why it inspires you. No need to reverse engineer the song. Instead you are going to use the song itself as a template for your own work.

Drag the song into a new music project. From here there are several things you can do. You can use the song structure and chord arrangement as is, or you can grab a certain section and loop it. I like to grab a loop and work with that, preferably an instrumental section.

What you'll do from there is simply play on top of it. Add your own melody, bass part, pads, and drums. Just keep building until you have the beginnings or your own song. Keep improvising on top of the loop for several minutes. Try to play something different that captures a similar mood for you. Later you will delete your ghost track and start picking out the good bits of what you've played. Soon, you'll be on your way to completing your own piece of music with rhythms, structure and melodies inspired by the original ghost track.

It's like having someone guide you towards something captivating and away from mental blocks. You don't have the same pressure of making all these little decisions, instead you are just jamming to something you already love. What a great state of mind to be working from.

Great music inspires great music

It would be no exaggeration to say that much of the music you love was inspired by a song or songs that the artist loved. Many great songs have simply borrowed another song's drum rhythm or chord structure. Sometimes a melody is hijacked noticeably, or sometimes it is altered just enough to disguise the original influence.

Think about how a genre of music is created. Do you think it's just a bunch of unconnected artists that randomly ended up in the same place? Well, maybe there is a minuscule percentage of these cases, but overwhelmingly, someone does something that sounds fresh and a bunch of other artists jump on that idea and do their own version. They "borrow" 90% of someone else's idea and put their own 10% twist on it.

But is it cheating?

This really depends on your idea of what cheating is. Where does cheating really start or end? If cheating is using someone else's hard work for your own purpose, then pretty much any tool is cheating.

The piano is a beautiful instrument that has wonderful tone when played a certain way, but can you really take credit for how wonderful it sounds just because you assigned chords and notes to it? You've got to admit that some of the magic is in the sound itself, even if you've tweaked that sound.

Then there are your recording devices, the software in your computer (or hardware), the effects, the mixing engineer and the mastering guy. That would be a lot to take on to make something completely original.

You can't take credit for the sound itself, just as a cook can't take credit for the knives he uses or even the ingredients. How many people have made lasagna, or an omelet? Even though people make them at least 80% the same, there are those minor details that makes an average cuisine amazing. Imagine how awful it would be if there was no theft allowed in cooking? There can be only one spaghetti sauce. Only one peanut butter. What a waste of a chance to improve upon a good idea. Often times the artist might consider the magic moment as a mistake or a failure, but may inspire a whole league of loyal followers unexpectedly. This is creative evolution and nothing can be more natural.

We are always standing on the shoulders of giants with anything we do creatively. Nothing is 100% original. We are using tools that are improvements of other tools and so on. The tools are constantly being tweaked and refined for different preferences. These tools allow us to inject our own skills into the process without having to reinvent every necessary wheel. We get to focus on our strengths while benefiting from the creativity of those who came before us.

I think this kind of borrowing and theft can be a wonderful thing, even though some theft gives more creative results than others. It allows us to fully explore a sound with different artists coming at it from a different perspective. There will always be hacks that don't really add anything to the pot, but then there can be a magic mixture that may only have a 2% tweak, but it affects us in a very positive and special way.

The whole art of music is really a process of imitation and tweaking to one's taste. This can pretty much be said for any kind of creative work. You learn the rules and then you break them. Are you trying to live on your own creative island or are you willing to interact with the magic that is all around you? I give you permission to join the party. I'm not giving up the ghost any time soon.

A simple but rarely used song writing and arrangement technique

This is a song writing technique that I almost didn't want to write about. It's so silly and obvious that I thought I might be the only person to find use with it. As I pondered it for a few days, this technique became more and more intriguing as a way to get ideas down and arranged quickly.

A common problem people have with song writing is sound design, programming and arrangement. This is because you constantly have to get out of your flow to try to dial in an idea. Often times this leads to you forgetting what you were trying to do in the first place. Once you've forgotten your original inspiration, everything you do from there is a bit of a shot in the dark.

If only you could lay down all your ideas in real-time without having to stop and lose your flow.

I'd like to help you do that.

Hum it out

Instead of going directly to your favorite drum kit and synth pre-sets and trying to get things dialed in, how about laying down a blueprint first. What I suggest is you put some headphones on and get a mic (or use your computer's internal mic). It doesn't have to be great, so don't sweat looking for the perfect one. Next tap out the tempo of the idea in your head.

Turn on the metronome, hit record on a track and beatbox/hum your song idea into the mic to the click track in your headphones. Try to record your song idea as one take even if you don't have it all worked out. You'll find that when you get into this flow, ideas just come to you. It'll be like you're making it up as you go along. You'll naturally create little variations, breaks, drum fills and interesting edits. It's ok to overdub over certain parts later, but just get a rough idea.

Now, you're probably thinking this is ridiculous, but stick with me. What makes this incredibly useful is that after the end of this exercise you'll actually have a structured song idea with breaks that aren't forced, because you put them there when they felt "right". You may have even come up with more clever rhythms and tweaks because you weren't limited by technology.

Another advantage is that there are only so many parts you can hum at once. You are mainly going to get "impressions" of the idea in your head, instead of a perfectly accurate depiction. This will also tell you the most important parts in each section, so you can keep things interesting without overloading your song with too much stuff.

Feel free to add another voice layer to fill in some details if you like. I'd imagine myself starting with drums and bass, and then let it go wherever it takes me. You'll naturally be humming the most "stand out" element of your song idea as you go.

Once you've gone through this process, you'll have a clear path to follow as you dive in to the more technical parts of creating your song without getting lost. You'll be able to now take the time to perfect your sounds in confidence. I think you'll find that different (and typically better) ideas come to you in real time, instead of with you poking in midi notes, trying to come up with that perfect drum fill.

Of course you don't have to stick with your original idea, but it still always helps to have a rough blueprint. Happy accidents will still naturally come, so don't worry too much about that. The song writing process will now just be matching the sounds in the computer to the sounds you had in your head using your "hum" track as a reference.

Until the computer is able to take ideas straight out of your head, this is the best I can offer. And heck, this is how Michael Jackson wrote most of his tunes. If it worked for him, I imagine it can work for you.

How being broke & having poor musicianship made me a better song writer

I started off on my musical path when I was broke. There was nothing glamorous about it. I truly had nothing but a burning desire to make music that didn't suck. I had no musical training to speak of (let's be honest, I still don't), so I wasn't a virtuoso by any stretch of the imagination. So there I was, no money and no talent.

To be fair, I did grow up around my Dad's studio in the back of the house for the first few years of my life, so there may have been some little things I picked up unconsciously, but I really had little interest in making music until I was fifteen. I first wanted to be a drummer (thank god that didn't happen. I'd have gone nowhere), then I wanted to play synths like Nick Rhodes of *Duran Duran*, but instead my Dad gave me a guitar and a cheap amp of his. Being that I had no money to buy something else, that's what I played.

My dad gave me a chord book, but after a few weeks of frustration I chucked it.

Having no musical training to fall back on, I had to find the easiest way to play songs. My solution was to disregard solos and just follow the bassline. In fact, when I started playing guitar, I just played one string at a time, picking up on simple basslines and melodies by ear. I didn't know any chords.

Eventually I learned that I could make a two string chord by adding the 5th on the second string. I played my first string of live performances like this. Luckily, someone pulled me aside and showed me how to add the octave on the third string for a fuller chord (without talking down to me or being condescending). From there I learned some bar chords, and experimented my way to discovering new ways to make sound. Since I wasn't a proper musician, I had to keep to what was simple and figure out the core of what makes a song tick. This is still the core of my music making today.

When playing with bands that had more talent than us, my bands still seemed to win the audience almost every time (to my surprise). This taught me early on that talent and good music didn't always have to go hand in hand. Sure, you have to learn to play your own songs well, but your songs aren't required to be hard to play to be good. This was liberating, and gave me the freedom to just play what sounded good to me regardless of the skill required to play it. I only became interested in upping my skill set when I lacked the skill to play something that was in my head. This allowed me to put all my focus on writing music, instead of figuring out what everybody else was doing.

I suppose if you wanted to be in a progressive rock band, you would probably have to be far more skilled than me, but the music I loved wasn't that complex, so I was able to fake it pretty well. Although my musicianship grew marginally, my song writing skills were improving by leaps and bounds since that's where all my energy was being focused.

As my interest in synths grew, I didn't have a whole lot of choice, because I was broke, so I had to buy what I could afford and try to get the most out of it. I'd save for several months, and eat a lot of Top Ramen in the meantime.

I ended up with three pieces of equipment that I used for the next 8 years:

A used Roland Juno 106

A Roland U220 synth module (128 sounds with very limited editing. 6 parts multi-timbral)

A Kawai Q-80 Sequencer (32 tracks of sequencing over 16 midi channels)

I'm sad to admit that I used the Juno more as a controller (without velocity control, mind you), then I did for its own fantastic sounds. This was mainly because it was easier to plug in my cheap headphones to the U220 and get writing. At the time I couldn't afford a mixer to plug both synths into, but I realize now that the easy set up kept me from any distractions.

I spent a good amount of time learning these pieces of equipment and learning how to program drums and use the sequencer, however, as usual, I only learned as much as I needed to move forward. I didn't bother trying to learn anything I couldn't put right to use. I considered that a waste of energy. I was aware that I was only using 30% of my equipment's potential, but when you are finishing songs, who needs the distraction?

Since I only had 128 sound choices and a few drum kits, there was very little I could do with the sounds, aside from layering and stacking them, I didn't get slowed down in sound design mode. Sure, I could mess with the attack time or add reverb, delay or chorus, but other than that, I had to work with what I had. This once again forced me to focus on what was essential for a decent song, and I realized that crazy sounds were icing on the cake, but not the cake itself. In the same way, a guitar solo is nice, but without a well-structured song to carry it, it's kind of pointless.

Now I admit that these days I find sound design a lot more important, and that sometimes a non-musical sound can be the hook in a techno song, but I haven't forgotten the lessons I learned when I had far fewer choices.

The main lesson I have learned from all this (even though I still struggle at times to follow it) is that simplicity is key to a listenable song. The listener wants to take an active role in how they interpret the music. The simpler it is, the more their own mind can fill in the gaps, making it a more pleasurable experience for a wider audience. I'm not saying that you shouldn't pursue new skill sets to put in your toolbox, but make sure it is adding to your music and not to your ego.

Now that I have a greater skill set, more money than I used to, and modern technology on my side, I have to remind myself what I am here to accomplish. Like everybody, I sometimes miss the plot, but I am incredibly grateful for the days when I was broke and clueless. It taught me the most important lessons for my own music making, which I still use to this day.

I hope you can find a way to experience this for yourself. It's more necessary than ever with distractions like social media, game consoles and 500 channels of crap to watch on TV. I'm sure you will find this experience humbling and powerful.

How I Write Songs

I wanted to share one of my processes for writing a song from scratch. I figure if I could give a breakdown of it, it might help you save some time, making their own songs. Some of this might be a bit technical, and understanding it might push you to research further in your DAW of choice or Google. I'm not purposely trying to confuse anyone, but rather wanting to go through my basic process in an unedited way. I'll do my best to be clear.

Where to start

Although I prefer starting with some sort of basic template of Drum kits, Bass presets and some effect chains (usually basic sounds that have created in a previous song), this section is going to assume you are starting from scratch.

This is pretty much how it all starts for most. I'll usually drag a reverb and a delay onto the two default return tracks. I'll add another return track for compression. This will be used for Parallel, or New York compression, which is basically mixing the fully compressed sound with the original. This has the advantage of adding punch and fatness without losing the transients. You also have control over how much you want to add to any of your tracks.

After adding the return tracks, I'll usually drop a midi Drum kit into a track to make a basic beat. I dial the sounds in as I go, but I usually want to find a groove with a good set of sounds. If you have any custom kits, feel free to use those. If not, just keep testing sounds until something catches your attention (don't overdo this process. Find a handful of kicks, snares, claps, hits etc & move on).

Once I have a working beat, I'll dial in the volumes, attack, decay, sustain and release on each sound. I'll use compression to try to get the most out of kicks and snares. Make sure you can process certain drum sounds individually, as you may want to add reverb to a snare & a delay to a hi hat but not affect the other sounds.

I may find myself dragging several more tracks or drums to layer with the original kit. Usually two to three sounds make up a kick or snare that I'm happy with, typically choosing which sound has the best low end, and which have the snap or high end. I'll then EQ out the low end of the sample that doesn't need it. Sometimes I'll use a low pass filter as well, to take off some of the high end frequencies, giving the drums a darker or dubbier sound. Other times I'll enhance the highs for a more aggressive sound. It all depends.

Bass

Next I'll dive into bass. Sometimes I know exactly what I'm looking for, but other times I haven't got a clue and I need to find the right sound before I know what to do with it. I Decide on whether I want a more analog or digital tone or a combination of both. Since I know *Operator* pretty well (in Ableton Live), it's easier for me to dial in a sound from scratch than with most other synths. With the other synths, I rely a bit on pre-sets as a starter point and the tweak to taste.

Another great bass tool is Spectrosonic's *Trilogy*. A huge range of great acoustic and electronic sounds. With some groove quantizing and good programming, you can get some pretty believable sounds.

If I am not already using a simple sine wave, I'll usually add that, just for the purpose of Sub bass. Then I'll back off the low frequencies of the other synth with a highpass filter. I may also back off the highs of the bass so it's not as aggressive (personal taste). If I later need more "bite", I may duplicate the synth and pitch it up an octave, knock out most of the lows and mids, and add a bit of distortion or saturation. I usually can keep this layer quite low, and it'll still have an impact on the overall sound. You can duplicate again, and add another layer pitched up a few semitones to create a harmonic if you want. I've found this to give me great results at times.

For drums and bass, I'll usually create a group for each, and add a subtle compression (2:1 or 2.5:1) just to make things get together. I rarely add reverb to my bass or the kick drum, but certainly use it lightly on other drum sounds if it helps to add depth. With drums, I find it important to have a combination of wet and dry sounds. The dryer sounds being the ones you want to stand out, while the others play more of a support role. I'll also try to remove any "mud" in my bass or drum sounds. I use a high pass filter to knock out anything unnecessary. I will also put a dip in the 350-650 Hz range to sharpen some sounds. This range tends to be where "mud" lives. A little subtractive EQ goes a long way.

Tuning

The next step I might take after getting my bass sounding good is to tune my drums to the bass. This is easier than it might sound, and there are a couple approaches that work for me. The one I use most is using an EQ effect, and sweeping the frequency with a thin Q and a lot of gain until the sound rings in harmony. Then I'll back off the gain, so that the tuning is a bit more hinted instead of in your face. I may add a second or third harmonic on the same sound if it seems to work. Another approach to tuning drums I learned from Ableton guy Dennis Desantis's misuse of the Frequency shifter. Using the fine tune can give some great results without ruining the sound.

Sidechaining

Sidechaining can be a godsend for much more than just making that dancefloor "pumping" sound. Used more subtly it can really help sort out places where the low frequencies of the kick drum and bass interfere with each other. I typically decide whether the low end of the bass or the kick is more important, and sidechain the other.

You can sidechain only the low frequencies and leave the higher frequencies untouched. This makes the effect much less noticeable, but improves the clarity of the mix. I may sidechain the hi hats to the kick for that typical pumping sound, as well as atmospherics and reverbs. This can really clean up your mix.

Another use is in mixing. Instead of automating one part down every time another part comes in, I'll just let the sidechain compressor push the sound down automatically whenever it hears the other sound coming in. I may duck a pad to make a lead or vocal sound clearer. I highly recommend you look into this.

Stab

Then next step I will usually attempt is some sort of Stab sound. Something with a fast attack and decay. This is the part that will play off the drum and bass rhythm. Often times reverb and/or delay can really enhance the sound of a stab. The goal is to get a good sound that cuts through the mix and doesn't screw up the momentum of the track. For an idea of a stab that really drives a dance song, look no further than *Lil Louis* – "French Kiss".

If you have an arpeggiated bassline, you might not need a stab. I'll usually create a four bar stab-like part just so there is a bit of variation in the pattern. Be careful not to lose the hypnotic quality of the part by changing things up too much (unless that is exactly what you are going for).

Pads, stretched tones

Pads or other long evolving sounds can be incredibly important. They give a track that loops a lot of movement and keeps the song from sounding too clean, which can often make things sound too mechanical, or even unprofessional. A great way to get a good pad or drone is to stretch the hell out of a sample, or pitcher down a sample in a sampler. Stretching vocal samples is a favorite of mine. It can sound so good so easily that it almost seems like you're cheating! I will typically add delay and long reverb to make it sound nice and wet, and to smooth the edges. This is a fantastic way to add some much needed atmosphere and movement to a track. Just make sure you are in the correct key. A simple pad layered with a stretched vocal or sound effect can give you excellent results.

Sometimes chopped up pads can make a very good stab or melodic hook sound if done correctly. *Sasha's* – "Xpander" is a perfect example.

Hook/Lead

At this point in my song writing I usually have to make a decision. Either let the song cruise along as is without a lead riff, or realize that it would seem lacking without it. In my 30 day music production Journal, I attempted several leads on a certain track but in the end decided it was better without them. This is a completely subjective thing, as your musical goals might be different than mine. As long as you are using your best judgement and you aren't just throwing parts in because they are "supposed" to be there, you should be in good shape.

Crashes/effects/reverse/cut ups

This is where I do a bit of filling in the blanks. I'll usually drop crashes and reverse cymbals in their logical places. Sometimes I just use these as markers to possibly be replaced by another sound. These will usually be placed at 8 or 16 bar intervals. Pretty obvious stuff, but it definitely makes a difference. Some artists don't use crashes at all. Listen to Daft Punk for example. If you can make it work for you, go for it. Personally, I've tried, but it's deceptively difficult to do what they do and still keep things interesting.

Once I've got the basics crashes and reverse sounds in place, I'll put atmospheric sounds with a good amount of delay, reverb or both in spots throughout the mix. Especially when a build or breakdown is needed. Without overdoing it, I just filled in the gaps. I check to make sure the intro part of the track isn't too empty. Although it's nice to save the good parts for later, you don't want any of your track to be boring. Using cut edits of parts that play later with some delay can give good results, especially if you are lacking hi frequency content.

Structure

This part is tough for most people. Even if you have been writing tunes for a while, structuring club music can still be challenging. For the sake of moving quickly and confidently through this process, I suggest you drag a song you like into your DAW of choice & borrow the structure. It's easy to see where the break points are visually, so just use that as a guide. People have been doing this for ages, it's not a big deal. You can always choose to extend or shorten sections as you progress through the song, so in the end, you are still in control.

Panning/EQ-ing/Mixing

Next I go through the mixing stage and dial in the panning for each sound. I may add an auto pan or automation to some sounds to give some random movement. This works well on atmospherics, while subtle panning is good for drum sounds that are otherwise stationary. I like to use a filter to give subtle movement as well. I may do a stereo spread of the upper frequencies of the bass, while keeping the sub frequencies mono.

Keep in mind that panning is also important for sounds with the same frequencies. Often times panning is more effective than EQ-ing to bring out a part's clarity. Unless I'm going for an artificial sound, I try to avoid extreme EQ-ing. For a more natural sound, start with panning and then attenuate unwanted frequencies instead of boosting frequencies. If you are using extreme boosting to try to bring out the bass in a sound, you probably should rework the source sound or just add a sine wave bass layer. You can't bring out something that isn't there to begin with.

When it comes to mixing, it's a good practice to listen to all the other parts besides the one you are mixing. It's very important to concentrate on how a part effects the totality of your song. If you do find yourself focusing on the part you are mixing, take it to where you think it sounds good, and then drop it back about 10-15%. If you don't get this habit under control, you'll end up with the newbie mistake of having the first parts you mix buried by the last parts you mix.

Mono mixing

Once I have a basic mix it's good to switch to mono, then turn off one of your monitors and get in front of it. Mixing in mono reveals phasing issues, if your effects are overdone, or if your panning is making a part less clear than it should be. Another great thing is that in mono, there is no "sweet spot". Wherever you are sitting, you'll get the same results. If you can get things sounding great in mono, you can be sure it'll sound excellent when back in stereo. Don't forget to return to stereo before mix down!

Editing for groove

Once I've made it this far, the first question I ask myself (when making music for clubs) is "Is this danceable? Does this make me want to move, or just stand in one place and nod my head?" There is nothing worse than a well-produced track that doesn't move you... or your audience. If I find that it isn't giving me the results I was hoping for, I inspect what part is slowing the track down. I first make sure the drums and bass alone get me excited, then I add parts one by one until the track sounds less danceable. Once I find the problem, I'll consider changing the rhythm or even pulling the whole part out. Then I'll continue adding parts, going through the same process. This can be frustrating after all the work you've put into each part, but it's important not to be married to any one part. *If it's not improving your song, it's making it worse.* Also it's not a bad idea to experiment with groove templates. They can make a pretty drastic difference in the vibe of your song.

Final tweaks

Some of these final tweaks can make the biggest impact on whether your song sounds great or just ok. Typically at this stage I've made a pretty safe mix. Everything has its place and nothing is taking up too much attention. That's a good place to be but not a great place to end.

It's important that you let certain parts have their chance to shine, so, for each important part, find out where that is. Once you introduce a sound loud enough to grab the listener's attention, they will hear it throughout the mix even when it's lower in volume. These little moments for each instrument gives your song more dynamics and constantly keeps your attention. A little boost goes a long way, so don't try to make ears bleed here, just make sure the listener knows when something new has arrived.

Once I've gone through this process, I'm usually pretty happy and I mix it down. Of course you want to make sure to play it on a few systems, do some a/b tests with songs you like the production of, and if necessary, fine tune your mix. I've been known to be "happy" with my mix, and still go back three or four times for final tweaks. Luckily this isn't all that bothersome because you know you are very close to finished and that's a great feeling.

Everyone has their own approach and all are valid if they work for you. Hopefully this has given you some ideas which I encourage you to use.

A minimalist approach to song writing

The more tools that people use for their song writing, the more that can potentially go wrong. This is not to say that tools can't be incredible time savers, but they can also be huge time wasters as well. What I want to share with you is a new way of thinking when it comes to writing and completing songs.

Preparation

- How long does it take you to "prepare" to make a track?

- Do you plan this out beforehand, or do you just fumble around for the right sample, plugin in, effect, synth, or synth preset during the song writing process?

- Besides all the sounds and effects, how many controllers are you setting up (or attempting to set up)?

- Are you struggling with getting hardware up and running in order to simplify your song writing process?

- Are you working with a midi controller or two? How often does it speed up your song writing process, rather than just giving you a prettier button to push to do pretty much the same thing?

I'm not trying to talk you out of using hardware or software tools, but rather warning you against trying to make everything "look" pretty and "professional" before you get started. This is a mistake myself and many other producers have run up against. Hopefully it will help to break this cycle for those who read and share this book.

Remember: This is your song writing time, this isn't your "*sound design, muck around with effects you've never used, try to get this damn controller working because everyone says how badass it is*" time.

All that stuff needs to be set aside for another time, a time that isn't devoted to writing and completing songs.

A DJ-ing Analogy

Think in terms of a DJ on stage, with a crowd ready for a great show...

- Does a DJ get on stage and *then* start trying to learn new tools?

- Does he think "Wow, I think I'm going to read the manual on this new effects unit I just bought"?

- Does a DJ think "Wow, this is a perfect time to listen to all those tracks I bought on Beatport to see what is worth playing"?

- Do they decide that *now* is the best time to prepare your song cues & loop markers?

Of course not!

A proper DJ presents a set using the tools and the songs already familiar to them. Even though there are 1000's of great tools available for DJ's, common sense tells us that regardless of how amazing some tool might be, it will only take away from the performance to use tools that are unfamiliar to you, and probably get you some strange "What the hell is this guy doing?" kind of looks.

This is the same way you should look at song writing....

Only look to tools you are familiar with

Although there are a *ton* of choices out there (and probably on your hard drive), your best results are dependent on using the tools that are tried and trusted to you. This is not the time to learn a new skill. This is a time to put the skills you have already learned to use. You should start with "go to" presets for compression, EQ, delay & reverb, as these are the essentials.

This one habit will help to build your production vocabulary, and also force you to put to use what you *already* know, instead of filling your head with more techniques that you aren't likely to use.

Another *huge* benefit is that when you hit a roadblock, you have just been shown exactly what it is you need to learn next!

Don't bother reading manuals or watching videos that you don't plan on putting to use right now. Why fill your head with information that is likely to be useless to you in this moment? Doesn't it make more sense to only gather new information when you have run into a problem that needs solving?

This is powerful for two reasons:

1. Your focus stays on your music and its completion
2. When you learn a new technique that you put to use right away, you get this great feeling of discovery. For you, this is a new world you have opened up. You haven't let it sit in your head and get stale.

Have a direction

This might seem obvious, but I can't even count how many times I've convinced myself to just "go with the flow". This (although it can create some magical moments and happy accidents) is usually a bad idea when you are in "song completion" mode. Going with the flow is much more of a sound design type mentality. A practice of open minded improvisation.

Believe me when I say that this is a powerful way to get inspiring nuggets that can become songs, but a mind in that mode tends to want to continue on that path instead of actually finishing anything. If you do this type of thing during your song writing time, make sure to set a time limit (I'd say fifteen minutes at a time), and make sure you are using a tool you are familiar with. You don't want to get caught up trying to teach yourself a new skill, when you should be using the skills you have to finish songs.

Repeat after me:

"I know enough *right now* to finish a song."

Now, *believe it.*

Your "to learn" list

When you find limitations in your song, take note and put it on the list of "things to learn". Keep this list to three things tops, and make sure to tackle those and put them to use before you add anything new to your list. This should become a sacred practice. Use what you learn as soon as possible. If you don't plan on putting a new technique to use, take it off your list. "This is really cool" is a completely different list, so don't get hung up on that. It only stands to overwhelm you with choices, and lower your confidence in the tried and true techniques you already know.

Take inventory

What works right now? I'm talking about things that don't need to come out of the box and be set up. Once again, what is working right now? What tools are you already comfortable with? If you are an ace at using one tool that does the job, don't dive into a newer program just yet. Yes, those tools are amazing, but they aren't going to be amazing for you *until you've learned them*. Put it on your "to learn" list and use those new skills on your next project.

During my last remix project, I bypassed all my controllers because they weren't making my life any easier with completing the track. I even bypassed my studio monitors because my sound card was acting up on me. This just left me, my laptop and a pair of good headphones. Although this wasn't the ideal situation, it was liberating to solve technical issues by simply not using what wasn't working. I worked at using my limitations to my advantage by cutting myself off from too many choices, and forcing myself to get to the business of completing my remix.

What do you have that works right now? Use what you've got, and keep working until you simply have no more workarounds. Only at that point should you take a break from writing, and teach yourself the one new technique or tool you need to move beyond your roadblock. I guarantee that this new tool or technique will become part of your vocabulary of production resources, instead of just idly sitting inside your head filling up space.

Use a reference

I can't stress this enough. Give yourself the time to get a rough idea of what you are attempting to accomplish. Find some songs that you'll want to use as references for the mood and arrangement you are looking for. Even if you have a 16 bar loop that you are happy with, being able to reference a completed song will serve to keep you on track, and get you past several roadblocks.

If you don't have any direction, then you are simply sound designing and experimenting. You aren't song writing. I am not denying the incredibly importance of experimentation, but rather attempting to keep you from losing focus and ending up with another unfinished idea that will never be heard or enjoyed by others.

Minimize your choices

Once you have a direction and know the basic sound and mood you are going for, it's time to prepare the tools for the job.

Ask yourself "what is the fastest and easiest way to get the results I want". Limit yourself to a couple reverbs and delays. Also have your drum kits, swells, reverse cymbals and "go to" FX sounds all ready to go (I personally have lost a lot of time by not preparing this stuff ahead of time... trust me on this one). Layout and name your tracks ahead of time with words that will give you direction (drums, bass, strings, melody, percussion etc.). Only use the tools you are already familiar with. Want to learn a new synth or plugin? Put it on your "to learn" list, and take the time to learn it after your current song writing session... For now, only use what you know. You can bring your new skills into your next session.

Presets

For many, the word preset is a bad word. I don't see this as the case. Presets are your friends, not your enemy. There are literally thousands of presets available to you and your own tastes dictate which ones you will gravitate towards.

There is an unlimited amount of variation in classical music composers, even though they are building their pieces from the same template of sounds. Don't get caught up on the idea of every sound having to be home brewed. Think of all the great original music constructed from sampling other people's music exclusively. Or think of how a great DJ takes the works of other producers and combines it together in a way that creates a new experience.

In essence, the artist is working with already made presets. Of course you are free to make your own effects and synth presets on your off time, and I highly encourage that, but you want to have some "go to" sounds at your disposal for quick access. You shouldn't have to mess around with a sound for too long before it sounds right for your project. You can always come back later to modify your work, or introduce a new technique that you previously didn't have available to you, but whenever you are in song writing mode, *use what you know.*

As you build your own custom sounds, make sure to save these to your presets for quick access in other projects. A great way to build up some custom presets is to simply name and save all the sounds you use in your other finished and unfinished song ideas. You already know that these sounds are attractive to you, otherwise you wouldn't have used them in the first place. This can really come in handy, and start you building your own "sound".

It's completely ok to have your own formula for song writing. You will always expand and evolve, but you'll be building from your past knowledge. Don't abandon your current skill sets just because you saw somebody do something really cool on You Tube, instead pick up a couple of tricks that you can incorporate into what you are already doing. By holding to your own identity, you won't run the risk of becoming a copycat artist that is always jumping on bandwagons but never developing his own personality.

The path of least resistance

Song writing itself is already a path of a lot of resistance. It takes quite a bit of determination to complete something you started. Completing a song forces you to own your creative decisions, and the best decisions you can make are educated ones.

Let your past experience guide your current creative flow, and let your current roadblocks drive you to new solutions, tools and techniques. Always aim for the solution that doesn't slow you down. Completing songs is a skill above and beyond all others. You will likely find that many of the guys with the coolest and craziest techniques lack the ability to actually finish something. Don't get caught up in thinking there is anything more you need to know in order to finish a song right now. Like with any skill, you will improve with consistent repetition and fine adjustments.

Finishing club tracks

Of all the roadblocks musicians run into, I would say that finishing tracks sits at the top of that list (or very near the top).

You are working on your favorite producing platform and you've got a rocking groove going on a 16 bar loop. You are moving and grooving but you can't seem to get yourself past this point. Every time you return to this track to finally get this song done, you end up just spending hour after hour listening to the loop and pondering each sound and component and at the end of the day are no closer to that elusive finished track.

If this is you, realize that you are further along than you may think. Especially if after a week or so you are still liking the groove you created. Below are a few thoughts that may help get you over that hump of countless unfinished songs and on the track to more productive song writing habits.

Don't wait for inspiration

Perspiration always beats waiting for inspiration. Why? Because energy in motion creates emotion, and emotion inspires you.

In other words, allow inspiration to follow a consistent work ethic. You will find that your mind tunes in to your habitual actions and will set your music as a higher priority. This will lead to being inspired much more often. When I started writing this section, I wasn't in the mood. I had to push myself to just start. But now that I've put my writing in motion, one idea after another began to pop up and it pretty much started writing itself. Don't think you have time to devote to regular music sessions? Why not take my thirty day challenge and see how it works for you.

Here's the url: bit.ly/3apRHGg

Samples vs. Sound design

Although there is nothing quite like creating your own unique sounds from scratch there are some things you might want to consider.

If you aren't an expert on designing your own sounds, this process can take you from inspiration to mental exhaustion. When you are trying to bang out a tune, speed is of major importance. You don't want to have too much time to ponder and second guess. You want to get in the flow and stay in that flow with as few distractions as possible.

Many of the successful producers out there don't seem to be great sound designers, but rather very organized and fast moving. They usually have many "go to" sounds, FX and presets. They often have templates ready to go as well, so they have an idea how the song will be structured in advance. They also use sample libraries for drum hits and drum loops just to get the track moving, and may change them later on.

Bass can be a pretty tricky business to get right, and often finding a preset and tweaking it will keep you from getting lost in sound design. As I have talked about before, it's important to separate your sound design time from your song writing time. Trying to do both in one session can really slow you down, or even bring your productivity to a screeching halt.

Create your peak first

The peak of a track is the point at which your song has the most excitement and energy. This is the point that all the other parts in your song reference and point to. This should be the biggest moment of your song (or the part that conveys the most intense emotions). This is the payoff you deliver from any break downs and build up's. If you don't nail the peak of your track, then you don't have a song.

Once you have your peak you can stop adding parts to your song, as more parts will begin to muddy up and drop the energy level you've just created. Usually this will also be where more parts are playing at the same time. If all your parts are working together in the right way and aren't conflicting with each other, you are half way home.

In many cases, the peak of your song is about 3/4 of the way into your track. This isn't a firm rule, but if you aren't yet in the habit of finishing your tracks, you may want to follow guidelines that have worked for others until you build your own confidence in completing tracks.

If you are having difficulty creating the peak of your track and can't seem to figure out what it needs, a simple solution is to find other songs in the same key, match the bpm's and play them together with your song idea (your song should be 6-10 dB louder than the songs you are mixing). When you hear something that grabs your attention and drives the groove forward, take note of it and mimic it in your track. Sometimes you just want the groove of the part, and in some cases it's just the sound your song needs.

Song structure

In its most basic form, the structure of a dance track is going to follow this format. If this format doesn't work for you, simply analyze the structure of a song you would like to emulate, like mentioned earlier in this book (page 136).

- *Intro (8-16 bars)* - Usually a simple beat that makes your track easy to mix.

- *Bass drop (32 bars)* - Like it sounds, this is where the Bass comes in. The intro gives the DJ time to transition from one Bassline to the next.

- *Breakdown/build up (4-8 bars)* - This is usually where the kick drum is removed, and a key melody or emotional aspect is introduced.

- *Meat of the song (32-64 bars)* - This is where the song really comes together and sets the tone. It should make you move, but not yet give you everything.

- *Breakdown/build-up 2 (4-8 bars)* - similar to the first breakdown, but may feature elements that make it even more intense.

- *Peak (32-64 bars)* - this is the moment everything lets loose, and the track gives you everything it's got. Typically after 32 bars, the intensity should back off a bit, like the way it was after the first breakdown.

- *Outro (8-16 bars)* - this is similar to the intro, and is there to allow the DJ to transition to the next track without conflicts.

Besides the intro and outro, each section should have something of interest happening every 4-8 bars (crashes, atmospherics, FX etc.) with new sounds being introduced throughout. To create more interest on parts that repeat, experiment with the filter, *lfo's* or effects on some of the parts. Even slight changes will keep the mind interested.

Less is more

When your goal is to finish a song, it's a good idea to get a basic groove up and running, and not get too nit-picky about all the details quite yet. In my opinion, it's a good idea to create your groove that will become the song, and then work out the structure of the song. You can always touch up the kick or bass tone once you see how everything else is playing off it.

Only after you've got the structure in place would I suggest you start putting in all the crashes, filters, atmospherics, incidentals and automation. Having your song structured will motivate you to finish the song more than an elaborate 16 bar loop will.

Solo each part

Nearly every part of your track should be able to stand on its own (in some cases, multiple sounds create one final sound). If you continue to feel that your track needs more and more and more, you may want to consider that the key components to your songs are not right and need to be replaced.

Try not to get your ego involved here. Sometimes that sound you spent ages on just doesn't work and a preset does. Don't get caught up in trying to force things. Maybe that sound can be used in another tune, but for now your focus is finishing the song in front of you. This also goes for over using effects and EQ to compensate for a lousy sound. It's much better to mangle a sound that is already great.

Steal, then replace

In the name of speed and keeping the process flowing. If you hear a sound that inspires you, whether it be a kick, a stab, or some atmospheric, just steal it and keep moving. You can go back later and recreate the sounds if you are paranoid of licensing issues (although most of the sounds you are stealing were already stolen from somewhere else).

I'm not saying you should just steal your way to success, but in the name of finishing your track, there is no point in spending a week trying to get that perfect kick tone when you can just steal it and move on to the next stage.

I feel that paranoia holds more musicians back than it ever serves. If you really feel your track is going to be successful enough to worry about being sued, you can always hire someone to recreate sounds for you later.

Partnerships

Many successful producers (especially DJ's) have a team of engineers and sound designers that can take a basic song idea and take it to the next level.

Unless you have the budget to do this, my suggestion would be to find a partner to work with who has skills that you are lacking and vice versa. This way when one of you burn out, the other can pick up the slack. With two or more people you can multiply your productivity. The power of two (or more) minds becomes much more than the sum of the parts.

EQ tip

When EQ-ing, unless you are going for an extreme effect, don't over EQ to compensate for a poor quality sound. Your song will practically mix itself if you are using the right sounds from the start. Over EQ-ing everything in sight is a sign that the content may be flawed.

How I wrote 49 songs in 1 year and how you can do the same

There is something to be said for taking on goals that seem bigger than you can handle. It this section, I'll be telling you exactly what I did and the results that came from it. Although some of this will seem like a decent amount of self-congratulation, I truly hope that this only reinforces what is possible for you if you commit and work consistently.

I am going to be as honest and candid as possible, as I want to share a realistic perspective on a topic that typically gets both over hyped and offers promises of easy success to all. That is both misleading and unethical, but hey, this *is* the music industry right?

The challenge

Unhappy with the results I had been getting with my music production, I made a decision to take on one of my biggest challenges. I knew I was serious and dedicated, because I didn't wait until the New Year to get started (it was in December).

I needed to know what could be if I actually gave this my best effort.

Aside from an indie dance remix for a favorite band of mine *West Indian Girl* (One of the vocalists would later marry Trent Reznor and form *How to Destroy Angels*), I had zero cred on Beatport. I would have to work my way up from the bottom.

After reading a fantastic book called "The War of Art" I had all the motivation I would ever have, so it was *go* time.

I decided I was going to commit to at least 1 hour of music making a day, every day, come rain or shine. To give myself public pressure, I created a free Facebook group just for this challenge, and invited anyone who wanted to join me to share their daily work as well. My goal was to create a support group of dedicated people just like me.

December was a tough month to get started, the holidays pulled me in different directions, and I had to be truly committed. I went twenty eight days straight without missing a day. Although I beat myself up a little, I'm pretty proud of that run. I wrote about 4-5 songs in that time from what I remember. My daily progress is still up on the Facebook page, but I would have to check it to be perfectly accurate.

My first songs I shared with my new friends at the P.U.N.C.H.I.S. club. Everyone said they liked my work except one of them, but what did he know right? Well, it turns out, his opinion would become the most important.

See, everyone who said they liked my stuff to my face secretly weren't feeling it, and told each other as much. When I found out, I had a serious talk with all of them to never spare my feelings when giving me feedback on a track. The feedback I would get from then on would be invaluable in developing my new sound.

I went through two revisions of the first song I was working on, and just wasn't hitting the mark. I could tell that my friends were losing a bit of faith in me, even though they believed in my skills as a producer. I had a choice, and I think this was a make or break moment. Was I going to sink into a funk? Was I going to just say "screw those guys" and do whatever I wanted?

No, I chose option three.

I sat down that day and started a new track, keeping in mind all the feedback I had received, and doing a bit of homework. In two days I had a winner, and it was the first track I had signed in five years.

From there, I had momentum and a new confidence that I could do this, and possibly even do it well.

By the end of the year, I had completed 49 original tracks, remixes and collaborations, and happily, I'm proud of most of them. In the past, I might have been happy with 20% of my work, so not only did my production output go way up, but also my satisfaction in my work.

Not a cakewalk

Setting any big goal is not easy, and this wasn't easy either. I had to put my producing above a lot of other business, while still doing my best to keep giving great value to my students and squeeze in a personal life as well.

Although I averaged at least an hour a day, sometimes spending up to 8 hours on certain days, I certainly found myself hitting burnout and taking the occasional day off. I seemed to be able to keep days off to a minimal until around September. Then I would start missing two days in a row. Missing three days once or twice was my worst run though. I contemplated just stopping for a couple of weeks, but chose to just keep fighting on.

I thought about author *Stephen King* a lot and how he is known for writing every single day (with the exception of his almost fatal car accident, and an attempt at retirement). His work ethic has always been an inspiration for me, and I've always wanted to do this with my music.

I often found myself mentally fatigued and having to just go through the motions and just pat myself on the back for beating procrastination for one more day. Sometimes that is the best we can do. Not all days can be inspired.

There were some points when a song I was working on was sounding like shit and I would get really down, and think I had lost it. I've found the best possible solution for this is to just work through it. I've found the shitty days usually only last for about three or four days before something clicks and gets you excited again. I ran into this probably three times over the year. Don't let it scare you, it's a normal part of the creative cycle.

Life and emotions will try to push you around through this process. You'll give yourself all the reasons in the world why you simply don't have the time. Your ego will soar and then hit the ground hard. You'll have to learn to give those voices in your head a heartfelt "Fuck You!" at times.

No matter what, stand up and take the next step.

Accomplishments so far

As I've stated before, this had been a stellar year. The most productive year of my life as a music maker. Hopefully you can see yourself in me, and realize that there is nothing stopping you from doing the same as me, if not more. From December to December I had completed 49 songs. This includes originals, remixes and bootlegs.

Out of these 49 songs, this is what was released on Beatport that year (and many more have been released since then)

- 8 EP's (with 5 more scheduled for release)

- 26 Tracks with my name on it (some are remixes of my tracks by other artists, so I didn't contribute to *all* of these)

- *Every* EP hit Beatport's Top 100 Minimal Releases Charts with some hitting the top 5.

- 2 tracks made Beatport's "Must Hear" charts.

Remember guys, this was a good 10 years after my peak with *Innerstate* (which was honestly only four songs, two of which got 99% of the support), so this was truly starting at ground zero again, and working nearly every day for a year straight. I really want to drill this into your heads. You can do this!

Below I will share some important things I have learned over this year that you can put to use *today*.

My advice for music producers

- Make music every day. This should be the obvious message by now, but I can't stress enough how much true experience you gain through daily practice. The parts of song writing that cause a lot of stress now will almost become automatic over the first couple of months. You will develop your own sound, and gain insights and intuition that no book you read can deliver. Where now it might seem impossible to sit down every day to write, daily practice will make it almost impossible not to make music.

- Borrow ideas from everywhere (including yourself). Anybody who is making a lot of music is allowing influences from all directions. Never shut this part of your brain down. Allow anything to inspire you, other songs, books, a conversation you overhear at a coffee shop, sound effects in movies, spoken word, nature, or the sounds of the city. Keep a notebook or audio recorder with you at all times. I can't tell you how many great sounds I got from recording the ambience of a diner, or randomly recording myself cooking in the kitchen. Just like with cooking, find great recipes and put your own unique twist on them. Everybody does it. Don't ever feel like you are cheating. You are cheating yourself if you close the doors to daily inspiration.

- Don't get married to one song, move on. Once you get in the habit of finishing songs (and if you work on music daily, you will finish songs), don't ever give your current song more importance than your next one. Finish a song, be proud of the accomplishment, and start a new song immediately. Don't paralyze yourself wondering if you can make a song as good as the last. Just get started. I promise good ideas will come when you make this a habit.

- Take notes. It's been extremely important to me to get myself out of the DAW and just use my ears to determine where I'm at with a song. Once I have a decent structure dialed in and I'm getting closer to the finish line, I'll render my song to a stereo mixdown and call it a day. The next morning, I will open up a notepad on my Mac and play the song through a couple of times, taking notes of what is working and not working throughout the song. I'll jot down the minute and second that I feel something needs to happen or if something needs to change. Sometimes I come up with as many as 20-30 little notes that I can immediately put to use after a short break. Sometimes you may need to repeat the whole process to make sure you've nailed it, and of course you should share it with a trusted person who can give you honest feedback. When you dive back into your DAW, your work will be much more focused, and you'll bang through things without all the second guessing.

- Buy music regularly. This is more important than you think. You can't seriously be a music fan if you don't support the artists you like with your own hard earned cash. You would expect the same when people come across your music. When you are supporting people with your money as well as your words, it will come back to you. People can see genuine vs fake supporters. You will also value the music you pay for much more, because you had to choose the very best tracks that you feel are worth your money. A much different process than the "download everything and see if anything is any good" approach. Trust me, supporting other artists will change you in many positive ways.

- Hire a coach. Nobody makes it on their own. Everybody has a team, even if it's a small one. Even Dirtybird owner Claude Von Stroke hired a coach, and it skyrocketed his results. Everybody needs to have someone to kick them in the ass at times and help them through certain struggles. I get coaching myself with my business and it gives me a 360 degree perspective of my situation and allows me to break down issues into easy to digest, bite sized tasks.

For people just getting started producing, a coach can help you get where you want in one tenth of the time. If you are pretty confident on the music front, it's not a bad idea to look into your time management, procrastination, focus, daily habits etc., and perhaps look into getting help in those fields.

Sometimes a great book can be a coach as well (if you actually read and *implement* its advice). Always think of ways to better yourself and your performance in as many areas of your life as possible. Sorting out life can make you far more creative, and help you free up time you didn't even know you had.

Equipment

Is buying new music equipment a benefit or a distraction?

I've found myself in circumstances in which I have really benefited from buying the right equipment, and other times I have purchased new gear as a way of delaying my own creative output.

Let's first talk about buying equipment...

When you are putting your studio together, there are simply going to be necessities that you can't get around if you want a good shot at getting the ideas out of your head with ease and enjoyment. The question typically comes up about what you should buy.

- Should you buy the most expensive piece of gear or can you get by with something cheaper?

- Does more expensive really mean better?

- Is this new piece of gear really going to benefit you, or are you just buying another toy that you will be bored with within a week?

From my personal experience I have suffered for *not* buying the right tools when I really needed them. Sometimes you get so used to shoddy tools that you consider all the extra trouble you go through to just be a normal part of the process. What you don't realize is that *what you are saving in dollars might be costing you pretty heavily in creativity, productivity and inspiration.*

When it came to my early productions in 1998, my production partner and I invested in a Pentium 2, 300 MHz PC. At the time this was pretty decent, but as technology leaped forward so did the minimum requirements of the software that was coming out. I can't even begin to tell you the amount of crashes, lock ups, and unsaved work that went down the drain.

On the other hand, when I decided to take DJ-ing more seriously, I spent the money and bought the best turntables, headphones and needles for the job. This made my life much easier, and also put me in the same mindset of the DJ's I admired because we were essentially working on some of the same equipment. It also made playing live much easier, since the clubs were stocked with equipment I was familiar with.

Another thing to consider, although you don't want to get too hung up on this, is *perception*. The way you are perceived can have a pretty big impact on your music career. If people see you working on substandard equipment, they may look at you as a person who doesn't take themselves seriously enough to invest more in themselves. I have found that investing in good equipment has more than paid for itself financially as well as in personal productivity. *Using good equipment is simply more inspiring.*

There is certainly an angle that I would like to put out there before I take things too far and have you maxing out your credit cards....

There is something to be said about using what you've got and getting the maximum productivity from it. *Norman Cook* (aka Fatboy Slim) has unquestionably been incredibly successful with his productions but are you aware that he did nearly all of those songs on an old Atari sequencer? This is a classic example of not buying into the hype of the "latest and greatest" and sticking to what works best for him. I'm certain however that he has an engineer that drops his work into Pro Tools or Logic and gives his work that polished finished sound we know and love.

All of this really comes down to knowing yourself and being honest with your purpose for purchasing new (or vintage) equipment. Is what you are purchasing really going to give your productions better quality and give you more enjoyment and productivity? *Have you become so afraid of creating that you are using new gear as a distraction from seeing what you are really capable of with what you've got?*

Be very aware that it's human nature to be in a constant mode of *"wanting"*. Having what we want rarely satisfies us for very long. Think of all the things you have bought that you almost never used. How many songs or full albums have you downloaded but never got around to enjoying? (I've certainly been guilty of this!)

If you are in the process of accumulating more often than in the process of putting what you've got to use, you might be stuck in an endless cycle & it's time to pull yourself out.

If you *must* get more gear (and everyone needs an upgrade at some point), a great idea is to buy one piece of gear and put it to use for thirty days to see if you really get good use out of it. If you don't, sell it. If you *do* really get a lot of use from it, great!

Now find something in your collection that you don't get much use from and pull it off your computer (you can always reload it if you later find use for it). You probably haven't used the thing in 6 months or more, but notice the sense of loss you feel as you remove it... Strange huh? This is a sign that you might have a kind of "pack rat" mentality and aren't able to let things go, even if you aren't using them. It's also a good habit to get rid of something old whenever you bring in something new.

Try something non-musical...

Go through your closet and pull out the things that no longer fit you, or that you simply never wear. Do you still have a hard time pulling it out of your closet and taking it to goodwill?

What are you settling for? Does your creativity call for better tools or are you giving yourself so many choices that it's stalling your creativity? Give it some thought and then do something about it.

Are you a creative consumer or producer?

In an attempt to become more productive you read blogs, watch videos and buy whatever seems to give you more power than you already have. The problem is that the appetite is never quenched. I'm of course referring to myself as well. I've been guilty of using information gathering as an excuse to not create. You end up in a constant cycle of feeding a part of you that never gets full.

Have you become an addicted consumer instead of a creative producer?

Now I am all about finding new information that I can put to use, but it can become an addiction quickly. We watch the videos, we read the blogs, go to the forums, but we are pulling in more information than we can possibly put to use?

A change in thinking

If this behavior is going to stop we need to accept that too much information works against you. It gives you too many choices. It also takes away your sense of discovery when you are in a creative mode. By the time you have a situation that would benefit from a certain technique, you may already be bored by it or paranoid that this trick isn't modern enough, or is overused, simply because you are already aware that it exists.

I think this behavior happens with a lot of musicians (something I've already stated that I am not). The reason for this is that many musicians learn *how* to play before they just start playing. They learn all the rules and they learn all the chords. By the time they actually start making music, they are trying to reach outside their current level of skill because they are already bored to tears with all the things they have learned. They restrict themselves from many of the basics in search of that *magic*, but rarely find it.

As I have mentioned before, I tried learning guitar from a chord book, but tossed it after only a few days. I had learned a few basic bar chords, and I was off and running. I wasn't afraid to do something just because it's easy. Luckily for me, I was drawn to bands that used simplicity in their favor.

If I had something in my head that I couldn't play, then and only then would I hunt for a new skill or technique, or expand my chord knowledge. This gave me the ability to feel the magic of every new discovery and tool. I didn't feel forced to grow any more than my natural pace. I rarely heard a song and had to rush home to learn how it was played. I was just doing my own thing and developing my own sound.

Being a producer or DJ, it's easy to get caught up with what is new; but it would be more beneficial if you put to use each new thing you learn. It's also going to be important to wait for a problem before you go hunting for a solution.

Ask yourself:

- Is this information I am going to use today?

- Does the project I am currently working on require this information to complete it?

- Does filling my head with this new information make me more productive now or less productive?

- What information do I have right now that I still haven't put to use?

- Might it be more beneficial to implement some of those one at a time?

Just because a technique is great for someone else and has them super excited doesn't mean it's going to work that way for you. Realize your addiction might be to someone's excitement, and not necessarily the information being presented. Another trap is trying to fit this new idea into your work. This can be frustrating and slow you down because in your head you may be thinking "This is supposed to be amazing, what am I doing wrong?", when the real issue is that it's not a match for *your* way of creating.

A challenge

Make a deal with yourself. If you spend thirty minutes learning a new trick, you've got to spend at least thirty minutes putting it to use. If the skill requires more time, decide whether you will dump the new trick or take the time to perfect it. Don't make the mistake of putting this on the back burner while hunting for new information.

Getting Signed

How to sign your music to labels

Below are some tips that are certain to improve your chances of signing more of your finished songs to labels.

They are just people

The very first thing I want you to understand, is that electronic record labels are not high & mighty entities. At the end of the day, it's just people trying to make a statement in the music scene. Labels aren't a whole lot different than artists, in fact, most of these labels are run by producers themselves.

With every label I have worked with or signed to, I can tell you this. None of the labels I have dealt with have been any more than a casual conversation. They want to know that you "get" their vibe & that their followers will buy what they release. It's really that simple.

Find the labels

So the very first step I would recommend to you is to search out the labels that will marry up nicely with your sound. Labels are very specific in their "sound" as it's the thing that makes them unique. Do not disrespect a label by offering them music that doesn't fit their sound. It'll just prove to them that you don't "get" it & they won't be interested in building a relationship with you as an artist.

If you produce & DJ, you probably already have an idea of which labels sound similar to your style. If not, try going to Mixcloud.com and hunt down mixes in your style & take a look at the artists and labels on their playlists. Often times, most of the labels will be of a similar vibe, so that can give you a head start.

Start small

I shouldn't have to tell you this, but do your best to keep your ego in check & realize that bigger labels rarely sign artists that don't already have some sort of reputation & some releases under their belt. Generally speaking, you should start small and build your way up. Smaller labels will be more open to new artists, as they aren't expecting to sell 5000 copies. Bigger commercial labels have to take all of that into account, so are less likely to pick you out of all the piles of submissions they get on a daily basis.

I'm not suggesting that you sell yourself short. There are some artists who *do* get signed to a bigger label right out of the gates, but I would assume that some kind of relationship was already in place. This is a very social scene & labels are more likely to sign friends than they are to sign a stranger. I'll get into that more later in this section.

Do your research

When you know which label(s) you want to aim for, you'll want to do some online research (google is your friend). Find out who runs the label(s) you are interested in & which artists are on the roster. Social media really becomes a blessing when it comes to building a relationship with these people, but you are sure to fail if you get ahead of yourself. You'll want to keep things slow and steady.

Do not introduce yourself as a music producer

This is a huge fail for anyone who wants to sign to a label. If you are hunting down label owners & sending them a link to your Soundcloud in your introduction, expect to be permanently ignored. If you have promoted yourself by commenting on other people's songs with "Nice tune bro! check out mine", quit it! You're failing.

The much better approach is to genuinely give a shit about the other artists & their success. Get in the conversations & know what you are talking about. If the artist makes a new release, and you like it, by all means, share it & comment on it. Don't just say "nice tune bro" (in fact, never use "bro" unless you guys are already pretty tight), instead say specifically what you dig about the tunes. This shows that you actually understand the artist's sound. That's important. It shows you are paying attention.

Do not give your constructive criticism on the artist's music. You're relationship isn't there yet. Any criticism should be private anyway and you shouldn't private message someone unless you have already been chatting publicly with the artist.

If you want a shot at a certain label, make sure the label owner sees you a lot in conversations with other artists the label associates with. Don't spam & don't share your music (although, feel free to share other songs you think the artists would want to add to their DJ sets)

Be confident, not arrogant

Never criticize yourself or your own music in conversations. Be able to look someone in the eye & say "this is good". If you can't do that, you aren't ready for a label yet. If you are apologizing for your music & lack confidence, how will you expect anyone to have faith in you as an artist?

Don't send unfinished demos to labels ever. Unless you have build that type of relationship, they have no time to nurture you or tell you what your song needs. You should consider your song finished before sharing it.

Find a production friend or mentor

It's always good to have a friend of mentor who "gets" your sound & can give you their constructive ideas to making your song sound label ready. It's as important as a writer hiring a great editor. I can't tell you how many of my songs have been improved, or completely saved from the trash bin by being open to advice.

This person shouldn't just be a buddy of yours. You need someone to tell you honestly when your music is not up to par, but at the same time a person who genuinely wants you to succeed.

Don't underestimate this step!

EP's not singles

When you are looking to sign your music, you don't want to think in terms of single tracks. These days labels are looking for an EP worth of music.

Most Labels want at least 2 original songs from you & will typically have 1 or 2 remixes, however other labels will want 4 or

5 originals. Understand the way a label likes to release music before submitting or you can expect to be ignored.

Get a Soundcloud account

These days, many labels research artists through their soundcloud, so you'll want to at least have snippets of your work & perhaps a few DJ mixes (not a bad way to get gigs). Some labels like you to submit them private links to your songs instead of downloads, so Soundcloud makes this really easy. Although I recommend getting a paid account, you can certainly start with a free account.

Have Patience

When submitting music to a label, you'll need to have some patience. Although some labels may get back to you quickly, others take some time. If you don't hear back in a week, check back with them. Some labels may not respond if they aren't interested. Don't sweat it, just know when to move on. There are tons of labels, so if your music is good, you are certain to find a fit.

Start your own Label

Many artists who found it difficult to categorize their sound specifically for other labels have had quite a bit of success at starting their own. Although this subject can be go petty deep, a great way to get your music on to Beatport, iTunes, Spotify and many others important places is to find a digital distributor. Running a label is hard work & is no way to get rich, but can be a wonderful way to get exposure & build your name.

Although it's not extremely easy to get accepted, it's easier than going direct to some of these digital stores. You'll typically want a 6 month release plan before going to a distributor. They want to know that you will be releasing at least once a month & that the quality will be consistent.

You may need to pay a remixer or 2 just to have a little name recognition for the label. That can help your label to get accepted. Here are a couple distributors you can look into.

Label-Worx

Symphonic

Essential Tips & Tricks

101 music habits & production tips for computer musicians

Here are some production tips & personal habits that I have implemented over my 24 year music making career. Some took me a long time to learn & caused me much more struggle & time wasting than necessary. I write this in hopes that I can help you increase your own productive output. You may make some connections to some common themes as I repeat things in different ways to drive important tips home. I hope you find some useful nuggets here.

EQ's

1. Use a hi pass filter (or a low cut) at 120hz or higher on every instrument that isn't kick or bass

2. Use a low pass filter (or high cut) on sounds that might compete with your hi hats. Usually around 7-8khz works well.

3. 350hz-650hz is typically where you find mud in your sounds.

4. To find offending frequencies (frequencies that hurt the ears or jump out too much), boost the gain on a narrow frequency band & sweep from low to high. When you high an offending frequency, lower the gain until it sounds better. There may be multiple offending frequencies, so you may need to use several frequency bands.

5. It's generally better to lower frequencies instead of boosting if you want a more natural sound & a fuller overall mix.

6. When boosting, it's better to use a wider frequency band. Narrow bands when reducing gain.

7. 11.1 khz is a great frequency to bring out hi hats.

8. Although boosting mids tends to make everything individually sound better, it will make for a cluttered, thin mix with no warmth. Choose wisely which parts you enhance, and choose a different frequency to enhance with each instrument.

9. Often times you'll have several parts fighting to be heard at the same frequency. It's best to choose which sound will highlight the lower mids & which one the upper mids. By sweeping the frequencies, you can find the dominant frequencies and chose a different one for each sound. Whichever frequency you decide to boost on one sound, make sure to lower that frequency on the other sound or sounds.

10. If you choose the right sounds, there is sometimes no need to EQ. Don't feel that every sound needs to be fiddled with.

11. Sometimes adding a bit of distortion or tape saturation to a sound can do a better job at enhancing a sound than EQ. Or sometimes a combination of both, just don't distort sub frequencies. Leave those clean.

12. A slight boost in the 12khz & above range can give your song a nice lift or air. Be very selective if you are doing this on individual instruments.

13. A small boost in the 1-6khz range can help bring sounds forward in the mix, while lowering those frequencies can place a sound a bit further back.

14. Avoid overusing the solo button when EQing an instrument. It doesn't matter how it sounds on it's own but rather how it sounds in the mix.

Compression

15. Kicks & bass can typically use stronger compression than other sounds but be careful if you are using samples that have already been compressed. No need to over do it.

16. Parallel compression can give you the best of 2 worlds by maintaining the original sound & it's transients while adding a tightly squeezed compressed layer. The best approach for this is to add a compressor to a send/return track. Set threshold to around -50db, attack as fast as possible, decay around 250ms & the ratio between 2:1 & 2.5:1. Then you'll be able to add a bit of this effect to any instrument you like.

17. Not everything needs compression, so allow certain parts to sit in the background. Choose your lead parts & supporting parts wisely.

18. Compression can give your parts more "click" or bite & shape the sound in several ways. Start with a high ratio, deep threshold & your release all the way down. First adjust the Attack, only looking for the "snap" or click, disregarding what comes after. Next adjust the release to help emphasize the snap & the body or the sound. Now you'll have an extreme setting so you'll know how the compressor is affecting your sound. now, lower your ratio to a level that sounds reasonable to you & bring up your threshold until you are happy with the results. If you prefer the extreme settings, that is fine too.

19. You can send a group of instruments to 1 compressor and a lighter setting (1.5:1-2:1) to help them "gel" together. This is helpful for drum layers that weren't all recorded together.

Mixing

20. When mixing a song, it's better to listen to every instrument except the one you are turning up, otherwise you'll tend to mix each part too loud & not notice how each part is effecting your mix. By the time you've mixed the last instrument, the first instruments will sound too low, which can become an endless cycle.

21. Check your mix in mono frequently. This will help you recognize phase cancellation & also help you find panning locations that make an instrument sound clearer in the mix.

22. Generally it's best to start with drums & bass & then slowly mix each part back in 1 at a time. If the groove is compromised or the bass loses it's punch, consider lowering, reworking or removing the part.

23. Check your mixes in multiple sound systems from your car to your computer speakers before you consider it done. Make sure to compare it to a high quality reference song that is similar to your sound.

24. When considering what to keep in a mix and what to chuck out, consider instruments in terms of frequency zones. If you have too many instruments in one zone & not enough in another, you might be able to solve both issues by playing an instrument in another octave. Otherwise you need to either do some sound sculpting with EQ's, so each part has it's own small zone or get rid of the part.

25. Keep in mind that your brain considers sounds with a faster attack or click (stabs, percussion) more important than sounds with a slower attack that kind of fade in (pads). If you want a pad sound to be more prominent, you may want to speed up the attack.

Arrangement

26. Although there are many variations to song arrangement, it's good to start by modeling your songs arrangement after another song you like. You can always change things once your find your inspiration, but this should help you build a song with confidence.

27. It's incredibly important to base your song on something of substance instead of diving immediately into all the tweaky effects. Always start with a basic groove, bass & chord structure. Only after you've build this into something intriguing should you start applying all the glitchy effects.

28. Make sure to create groups for each type of instrument so things stay organized. For example, group all your drum & percussion sounds together, bass sounds together, vocal tracks, pads & effects. Whatever works for you to keep you organized will save you a lot of time.

29. If you are using external instruments with midi, convert those to audio. This will help you avoid any syncing issues & give you greater editing options. You may also want to convert your internal midi instruments as well.

30. If your DAW has a "freeze" function, freezing your tracks can free up your computer's CPU.

Panning

31. It's generally a good idea to pan your instruments before you EQ. This is because the sound of an instrument can change not only by it's placement in the stereo field, but also the other instruments in the same panning area. Sometimes panning can solve frequency clashing issues without the need for much EQ.

32. Although certain instruments typically sound best in the center (kick, bass, vocal, snare, high hats), it can really help each instrument be heard to have a few ticks of separation between them. For example, I might put my snare 2 or 3 ticks to the left & high hat 2-3 ticks to the right.

33. Atmospheric reverbs can be panned hard left & right to give your song a wide sound.

34. For hard left & right pans of one instrument (guitars sometimes comes to mind), I like to duplicate the track, throw one left & the other right, but offset one by about 10 ms or until you hear the separation more clearly.

Sampling

35. To get a more vintage grit of the old hardware samplers, try bit reducing your sounds to 8 or 12bit with a sampling rate of 10-20khz.

36. Don't worry about a sample being clean enough. Dirty is good. If it sounds good to you, use it.

37. Even though it's good to have quality samples, It's also fine to sample from an mp3. It will usually sound better than old vinyl anyway. Just make sure most of your instrumentation is higher quality to balance out the final result.

38. When using short repeating samples, especially in drum sounds, it's important to add a bit of variation in volume, decay times & pitch.

39. A good way to extend a sampled sound like strings or a pad is to first make sure you are only sampling 1 note (meaning only 1 pitch, not a melody or changing chord). You don't want to sample multiple notes. Next, make sure you start the sample after the initial attack and end it before it fades. Lastly, if your sampler has this feature, set it to play the sound forward & then in reverse non-stop as you hold a key downer. Your sampler may also have "fade" or loop settings to smooth out the edges. This will create a pretty seamless sample. Alternatively, you can just place the sample in your software's arrangement window and duplicate the file to play forward & then reverse for whatever length you desire.

40. Sample from anything that inspires you. Movies, spoken word, the sounds of nature, factory machines & other songs. Repurposing sounds is an art unto itself. It doesn't matter where you take your ideas from, it's where you take them to. Worry about the legal side of things after you've created something beautiful.

41. By layering a sampled loop with a reverse phased copy of itself, you can often get clean sounds in the left & right speakers that were previously obscured by bass or vocals. This is a great way to make use of samples you might otherwise find unusable. It doesn't always work, but when it does, it gives you access to some pretty cool sounds.

Sidechaining

42. Sidechaining is a great way to keep your kicks sounding clean & give your parts a rhythmic "pumping" sound. To do this you'll need a Compressor plugin that is capable of sidechaining. You will drag the compressor to the track you want to add that "pumping" sound to & then there will be an option to choose what track to sidechain from. Typically people like to sidechain to a kick drum for the classic sidechain sound, but you can get really creative by trying other instruments to sidechain to. The setting on your compressor will usually have the threshold between -30 & -50db, ratio around 5:1, a fast attack & the decay between 150-350ms. Adjust the decay until you get the right timing & feel. Adjust the threshold for a more or less dramatic effect.

43. Sidechaining can also be a great mixing tool. Lets say your guitar and vocal are fighting for frequencies. You can simply sidechain the guitar to the vocals so that anytime the vocal come in, it will either lower the guitar volume, or lower the conflicting frequency of the guitar. This trick can really be a lifesaver for cleaning up your mixes.

Sends/Returns

44. A send/return allows you to add the same effect to multiple instruments in different amounts. It also saves on cpu usage since it's only 1 effect being run to multiple tracks.

45. Sends and returns are great to use on for common effects. Reverbs & delays especially. Make sure any effect on a return is 100% wet.

Groove

46. Quantizing can be a blessing or a curse. If your DAW of choice has groove quantizing or a randomizing feature, use subtle amounts to give it a more human feel.

47. If possible, play some parts by hand without quantizing. Ears perk up when they hear imperfect human playing (as long as it isn't way off of course)

48. In most DAWs these days, you have the ability to analyze the groove of a drumloop or a few bars of a song & apply it to your own work. Groove can powerfully impact the danceability or vibe of your song. It's not something you always hear, but you definitely feel it.

Drums

49. It makes good sense to add a subtle reverb to all your main drums so they sound like they were played in the same room, even if you plan on using a longer reverb on certain sounds. Careful with the kick though. You want your kick to remain as clean as possible.

50. Percussion sounds can have more impact in a mix if they are dry. Especially if other sounds have reverb.

51. It's a good idea to have several drum kits that are General Midi compatible. This makes it much easier to switch between kits without having to reprogram the midi notes. This also gives you the ability to borrow the drum programming from another song's midi file, which are pretty easy to hunt down on the internet.

Reverb

52. Reverb can be used to help give your track a greater rhythmic impact. The trick is to adjust the decay of the reverb to fade out right before the next 1/4 note (or 1/2 note) comes in. This will create another element of rhythm and can have a dramatic impact on your song's groove.

53. Use a predelay to give your instruments dimension while not losing the clarity, or as an interesting delayed sound. Works great with drums.

54. For most sounds you add reverb to, you'll want a highpass filter to remove low frequency reverb. You want to keep those low frequencies as clean as possible.

55. Reverse reverb can be a really cool effect and it's not hard to do. Simply reverse a sound. Apply 100% wet reverb to the reverse sound. Render the resulting sound. Re-import the sound as a layer to your original sound.

56. Avoid reverb on your kicks unless it's a special effect or the beginning of a breakdown.

57. Reverb plays a huge role in giving your song dimension & depth. By using different settings for certain instruments, you are able to make some things appear close (little to no reverb) to sounds that appear distant (longer reverbs, bigger rooms). It's a good idea to set up multiple send/return tracks with reverbs specifically dialed in for front, middle and rear of your mix.

58. Your "front" reverb should be set to have bright early refections & a shorter decay.

59. For a "rear" reverb, go for a darker sound by adjusting the high frequency damping & with a longer decay. You'll still want a high pass filter set to 100-120hz.

60. There are several types of reverbs & each plays a different role & gives a different sound. There is Plate reverb, spring reverb, convolution, chamber, hall, room & reverse. Feel free to use this link as a quick reference http://www.musicsoftwaretraining.com/blog/2011/04/27/how-reverb-works/

61. Here's a reverb trick used in Star Wars & others to double the apparent size of a room. Sometimes you just don't have access to a large enough room for the reverb you're looking for. The trick is to first record your sound dry. Now let's say we have a room that is 20x20x20 & we want to create the sound of a 40x40x40. You would record the sound being played in this space at twice the original speed (you can do this by sampling the original sound & playing it an octave up). You then take the results & play it at 1/2 speed. This will return the sound to it's original sped & pitch and give you the illusion of a much larger space. Finally layer this reverb with the original sound and the effect is complete. Real reverb, no plugins.

62. Increasing reverb decay times can create a nice building up feeling. Pulling back the reverb quickly can put a song back in motion & re-energize your song. Especially useful in club music.

Delay

63. Adding a subtle triplet delay to a simply melody can create more depth and complexity while adding to the overall groove. Works great for percussion too.

64. Replacing some of your reverbs with delay can help clean up your mix as delay is less dense. The delays should be a straightforward 1/4 note or 1/2 note instead of an unusual timing.

65. Like reverb, it's best to remove the low frequencies of your delays to keep your mix sounding clean.

66. Experiment with putting the delays wet/dry above 50% to create odd but sometimes very interesting timing changes of your parts.

67. A long delay followed by a filter with an lfo sweeping frequencies can create great atmospheric extras to your music. This works best as a send/return track. You'll also want the low frequencies removed.

68. Just so we're clear, delay should be avoided on sub bass frequencies

Layering

69. Most cool sounds you hear in a club track are multiple sounds layered together. Don't expect to recreate it with 1 sound. Use one layer to dial in the lows, one for the mids and another for the highs. EQ appropriately to make room for each layer. Add a little compression to help them gel together as one sound.

70. Duplicating a sound and pitching it up or down an octave can really help a sound stand out. This duplicated track usually doesn't have to be very high in volume to make an impact. In fact, subtle is probably better.

Bass

71. When it comes to mixing bass, louder is not necessarily better. If you push the bass too hard, you'll lose clarity in your mix. If you play the mix in your car and you can't hear anything but thump thump, you know why.

72. For electronic music, pretty much any bass sound will benefit from a sine wave taking up 120hz & below area. Make sure to put a high pass at 120hz on your main bass sound.

73. Much like kick drums, the "bite" in your bass is typically at around 1-3khz. This frequency helps the bass cut through the mix, so try boosting those frequencies a bit before boosting your whole bass volume.

74. Pitched down 808 kicks can make a great tone for a sub bass tone. Experiment with a slower attack as well.

75. Keep the sub frequencies mono even if you are using stereo on the upper frequencies.

76. You typically don't want lots of sub on both your bass & your kicks if they are playing at the same time. it's best to eq one for the sub frequencies and the other for the higher bass frequencies. This will make a cleaner mix and a much better sounding low end.

77. Bass getting lost in the mix? Try adding a second layer with just a click sound that hits at the beginning of every bass note. Wooden or metallic percussive samples with a very quick attack & decay work really well. Slight variances in the click can add more realism as well.

78. If you are using bass samples, make sure they have a solid low end to start with. Trying to boost bass EQ's won't help if there is nothing there to start with.

79. Duplicating your bass track & playing the same part in a higher octave can add richness to your bass sound. You will generally keep this layer lower in volume.

Sound design

80. Slightly detuning 2 oscillators with the same wave type (sine, square, saw etc) creates a thicker sound with a slight chorus effect. Great for pads but worth trying on just about anything.

81. It's much better to know 1 or 2 synths inside & out than barely knowing 50 synths. Take the time to choose one synth & go deep with it.

82. Remember that complex sounds are produced from simple sounds layered together. As you get to know your wave forms & different way you can alter them, it will become easier to reverse engineer them. The sooner you embrace the basics, the easier it will be to obtain the complex tones that excite you.

83. Spend time with a synth or other instrument just recording yourself making interesting sounds. Let go of the need to make music during these sessions & just record yourself playing around & exploring new sounds. You'll find plenty of great sounds you can cut up & use when you're back in writing mode.

84. Don't do your sound design & songwriting on the same day. It's better to let your mind go without any worries when creating sounds, while songwriting requires more focus & technical brain functions. Separating these habits will give you more productive results with both.

85. An LFO (low frequency oscillator) can add character to an otherwise boring sound. LFOs can control volume, pitch or filter (& many more parameters) changes at a chosen speed. Subtle amounts of LFO can add complexity and richness while more extreme settings can create different sounds altogether. Experiment with these as you make synth sounds or work with a sampler.

Other Tips

86. Close your browsers & turn off the internet when working on music. This way when you get distracted & try to jump on to Facebook, you'll be quickly reminded that you are in work mode & will get back on task.

87. If you have trouble staying focused, work in 30 minute blocks by setting a timer & committing to work for the full 30 minutes. After that you can stop, take a quick break or recommit for another 30 minute block. You'll be surprised how effective this can be.

88. Ghost tracks are a common secret among producers. The basic idea is to grab a loop or section from a song you like and start playing along to it. As you add more of your own layers, you will soon be able to delete the original loop and carry on building your song with the essence of the ghost track still remaining yet still completely your own.

89. Recording things with a microphone around your house or outside can make for some incredibly usable & unique sounds for your music. Go around and tap everything & bang things around in the kitchen. It can be an endless source of inspiration.

90. Without fail, long sounds rising or dropping in pitch, filter sweeps & reverse sounds can add drama & anticipation to a song. Building up white noise with a low pass filter is a standard for many club moments.

91. If you want to finish more songs, start with an idea on a simple instrument (piano, guitar, or bass). It's better to have a basic song structure in mind before you start. Think of it like a blueprint. This will keep you focused instead of getting lost wanking on effects and synth tweaks.

92. Don't start each song from scratch. It's best to create a template with send/return effects you're likely to use, a starter drum kit that sounds good & some bass and synth sounds at

easy access. You can change them later but templates help you get started quickly.

93. Don't judge yourself by the opinions of others who don't understand you & your art.

94. Don't keep adding parts to your track hoping it will solve your problems. If the basic elements don't inspire you, you probably want to rework those before adding anything new.

95. Steal & replace - Instead of agonizing over a kick sound, just sample one from a sample CD or record & move on. You can replace it with your own sound later, but don't lose your songwriting momentum doing sound design.

96. Be ruthless - Avoid getting married to a sound just because you spent a lot of time on it. If it's the weak link in your track. Ditch it.

97. There is no magic plugin. Get really familiar with what you've got & trust that this is enough. Your own limitations are what make you sound like you.

98. Take time to make the first elements of your song sound inspiring, whether it be adding little details to your drums or coming up with a great chord structure. This is important, as the rest of your tune will be inspired by these parts. Failing to do this can result in you realizing that no matter how much time & how many layers you put into a song, it's not going to excite you or the listener.

99. Don't only listen to the style of music you create. Original ideas come from outside influences. Try to make it a point to listen to a full album in a different genre of music once a week. Even a style you might not prefer. You're sure to have a much richer musical palette to draw from.

100. Collaborating with other artists is one of the best ways to boost your knowledge & gain some powerful production techniques. It's best to work with someone who has strengths where you have weaknesses.

101. Work on 1 song at a time. Don't build a cool sounding riff or 16 bar loop & then abandon it to start another idea. You'll never finish anything, and finished songs is all anyone cares about, not how much time you've spent in the studio. If you don't push through songwriting obstacles right when you come across them, you'll never gain the skills that will make you more productive on future songs.

And I'll leave you with an important final rule:

All rules are made to be broken

Thank You

I really appreciate you taking the time to explore The Mental Game. I hope this book gives you that extra push to get your art out into the world. It is my joy & honor to be of service in helping you take what is inside you & share it with the world.

If this book resonated with you & you are interested in working with me more directly, don't hesitate you drop me an email. I read every one of them. Jason@MusicSoftwareTraining.com

About the author

Jason Timothy teaches Music Production & Ableton Live on his website http://www.MusicSoftwareTraining.com

You can find his music on Spotify as **Jason Timothy** & also **Shhadows**

If you enjoyed this book, please give it a review on http://amazon.com/

Reviews   help   authors   immensely!

Resources for Ableton Users:

Producer's Playground

A huge resource of Video Courses, Tools, Templates
& instruments to take your music making to the next level,
backed by a supportive community.

MusicSoftwareTraining.com/playground

Create an EP in 30 Days
Master Course

Intense training over 30 days teaching you
the complete process to producing music in
your own style. This is exactly how I finished &
signed 52 songs in 13 months.

To join the next EP30 event, join the
waitlist at the link below:

MusicSoftwareTraining.com/waitlist

Private Coaching

If you are interested in personal coaching,
schedule a free consultation at the link below,
answer a few questions & book your session

MusicSoftwareTraining.com/Application

Made in United States
Troutdale, OR
10/31/2024